THE BOOK O
THE PROPHET

TRANSLATED FROM

RICHARD LAURENCE

1883

CONTENTS

INTRODUCTION

In the Authorized Version of the Epistle of Jude, we read the following words:—

"Enoch also, the seventh from Adam, prophesied of these, saying, Behold, the Lord cometh with ten thousands, of his saints, to execute judgment upon all, and to convince all that are ungodly among them of all their ungodly deeds which they have ungodly committed, and of all their hard speeches which ungodly sinners have spoken against Him."[1]

Modern research sees in the Epistle of Jude a work of the second century: but as orthodox theologians accept its contents as the inspired utterance of an Apostle, let us diligently search the Hebrew Scriptures for this important forecast of the second Advent of the Messiah. In vain we turn over the pages of the sacred Canon; not even in the Apocrypha can we trace one line from the pen of the marvellous being to whom uninterrupted immortality is assigned by apostolic[2] interpretation of Genesis v. 24. Were the prophecies of Enoch, therefore, accepted as a Divine revelation on that momentous day when Jesus explained the Scriptures, after his resurrection, to Jude and his apostolic brethren; and have we moderns betrayed our trust by excluding an inspired record from the Bible?

Reverting to the second century of Christianity, we find Irenæus and Clement of Alexandria citing the Book of Enoch without questioning its sacred character. Thus, Irenæus, assigning to the Book of Enoch an authenticity analogous to that of Mosaic literature, affirms that Enoch, although a man, filled the office of God's messenger to the angels.[3] Tertullian, who flourished at the close of the first and at the beginning of the second century, whilst admitting that the "Scripture of Enoch" is not received by some because it is not included in the Hebrew Canon, speaks of the author as "the most ancient prophet, Enoch," and of the book as the divinely inspired autograph of that immortal patriarch, preserved by Noah in the ark, or miraculously reproduced by

[1] Compare Book of Enoch ii.
[2] Heb. xi. 5.
[3] "Against Heresies," iv. 16. Compare Book of Enoch xv.

him through the inspiration of the Holy Spirit. Tertullian adds, "But as Enoch has spoken in the same scripture of the Lord, and 'every scripture suitable for edification is divinely inspired,' let us reject nothing which belongs to us. It may now seem to have been disavowed by the Jews like all other scripture which speaks of Christ—a fact which should cause us no surprise, as they were not to receive him, even when personally addressed by himself." These views Tertullian confirms by appealing to the testimony of the Apostle Jude.[4] The Book of Enoch was therefore as sacred as the Psalms or Isaiah in the eyes of the famous theologian, on whom modern orthodoxy relies as the chief canonist of New Testament scripture.

Origen (A.D. 254), in quoting Hebrew literature, assigns to the Book of Enoch the same authority as to the Psalms. In polemical discussion with Celsus, he affirms that the work of the antediluvian patriarch was not accepted in the Churches as Divine; and modern theologians have accordingly assumed that he rejected its inspiration: but the extent to which he adopts its language and ideas discloses personal conviction that Enoch was one of the greatest of the prophets. Thus, in his treatise on the angels, we read: "We are not to suppose that a special office has been assigned by mere accident to a particular angel: as to Raphael, the work of curing and healing; to Gabriel, the direction of wars; to Michael, the duty of hearing the prayers and supplications of men."[5] From what source but assumed revelation could Origen obtain and publish these circumstantial details of ministerial administration in heaven?

Turning to the Book of Enoch we read: "After this I besought the angel of peace, who proceeded with me, to explain all that was concealed. I said to him, Who are those whom I have seen on the four sides, and whose words I have heard and written down. He replied, The first is the merciful, the patient, the holy Michael. The second is he who presides over every suffering and every affliction of the sons of men, the holy Raphael. The third, who presides over all that is powerful, is Gabriel.
And the fourth, who presides over repentance and the hope of those who will inherit eternal life, is Phanuel."[6] We thus discover the source of

[4] "On Female Dress," ii.
[5] "De Principiis," viii.
[6] Book of Enoch xl. 8, 9.

Origen's apparently superhuman knowledge, and detect his implicit trust in the Book of Enoch as a Divine revelation.

When primitive Christianity had freely appropriated the visions of Enoch as the materials of constructive dogmas, this remarkable book gradually sank into oblivion, disappeared out of Western Christendom, and was eventually forgotten by a Church, which unconsciously perpetuated its teaching as the miraculous revelations of Christianity.

The Book of Enoch, unknown to Europe for nearly a thousand years, except through the fragments preserved by Georgius Syncellus (circa 792, A.D.), was at length discovered by Bruce in Abyssinia, who brought home three copies of the Ethiopic version in 1773, respecting which he writes: "Amongst the articles I consigned to the library at Paris was a very beautiful and magnificent copy of the Prophecies of Enoch, in large quarto; another is amongst the Books of Scripture which I brought home, standing immediately before the Book of Job, which is its proper place in the Abyssinian Canon; and a third copy I have presented to the Bodleian Library at Oxford, by the hands of Dr. Douglas, the Bishop of Carlisle."

This priceless manuscript, destined, some day, to reveal the forgotten source of many Christian dogmas and mysteries, rested in Bodleian obscurity, until presented to the world through an English translation by Dr. Laurence, Archbishop of Cashel, formerly Professor of Hebrew at Oxford, who issued his first edition in 1821, in apparent unconsciousness that he was giving to mankind the theological fossils through which we, in the clearer light of our generation, may study the "Evolution of Christianity."

The scarcity of Archbishop Laurence's translation, before the publication of the second edition in 1833, produced an impression in Germany that the work had been suppressed by its author; but this report is contradicted in the preface to the third edition, issued in 1838, in response to a large order from America.

The Book of Enoch excited more interest on the Continent than in England. It was translated into German by Dr. Hoffman in 1838, into Latin by Gfrörer in 1840, again into German by Dillmann in 1853, and has been discussed by Weisse, Lücke, Hilgenfeld, and Kalisch, the latter of whom uttered the prediction, that the book of Enoch "will one day be employed as a most important witness in the history of religious dogmas." The day and the hour have come, the clock has struck, and in thus publishing an edition of Archbishop Laurence's translation of the Book of Enoch, we place within the reach of all readers of the English language, the means of studying the pre-Christian origin of Christian mysteries.

Turning towards the "Preliminary Dissertation" of Archbishop Laurence, in which he discusses, with impartial criticism and accomplished scholarship, the origin of the Book of Enoch, we find him attaining the important conclusions, that it was written by a Jew of the Dispersion in his own language, whether Hebrew or the later Aramæan acquired in exile; that the version in the hands of the author of the Epistle of Jude and the Ante-Nicene Fathers was a Greek translation; and that the Ethiopic edition, whether translated from Aramæan or Greek, is the same work as that cited by the Apostle.

In attestation of the theory of an Aramaic or Syro-Chaldæan origin, Archbishop Laurence refers to the "most ancient remains of the Cabbala (Hebrew traditions) contained in the 'Zohar,' a species of philosophical commentary upon the Law, combining theological opinions with the allegorical subtleties of the mystical school. In this celebrated compilation of what was long supposed to constitute the hidden wisdom of the Jewish nation, occasional references are made to the Book of Enoch, as a book carefully preserved from generation to generation." Archbishop Laurence then gives extracts from the "Zohar," referring to important passages in the Book of Enoch, and infers that "the authors of the Cabbalistical remains wrote their recondite doctrines in Chaldee," and possessed a copy of the Book of Enoch, written in that language or in Hebrew, "which they regarded as the genuine work of him whose name it bore, and not as the spurious production of a later age."

Archbishop Laurence then considers the probable date of the work, and infers, from the quotation of Jude, that it must have been written antecedent to the Christian era, but not before the Captivity of Babylon, because it contains the language and imagery of Daniel, "in the representation of the Ancient of Days coming to judgment with the Son of man." But since Archbishop Laurence wrote, modern criticism has disclosed how nebulous is the date of Daniel, so that it becomes as reasonable to assume that the author or compiler borrowed from the Book of Enoch, as to attribute plagiarism to the pseudo-patriarch. The learned translator, however, discovered more satisfactory proof, through internal evidence, that the book "was written long subsequent to the commencement, and even to the conclusion, of the Babylonian Captivity."

That section of the Book of Enoch, extending from chapter lxxxii. to xc., contains an allegorical narrative of the royal dynasties of Israel and Judah, from which Archbishop Laurence constructs a history extending from Saul to the beginning of the reign of Herod the Great, and infers that the Book of Enoch was written " before the rise of Christianity; most probably at an early period of the reign of Herod." The Archbishop adds: "That it could not have been the production of a writer who lived after the inspired authors of the New Testament, or who was even coeval with them, must be manifest from the quotation of St. Jude—a quotation which proves it to have been in his time a work ascribed to Enoch himself."

Archbishop Laurence, furthermore, attains probability of date through another line of argument. In chapter liv. 9, of the Book of Enoch we read, "The chiefs of the East, among the Parthians and Medes, shall remove kings, in whom a spirit of perturbation shall enter. They shall hurl them from their thrones, springing as lions from their dens, and like famished wolves into the midst of the flock." Commenting on this passage, Archbishop Laurence says, "Now the Parthians were altogether unknown in history, until the 250th year before Christ, when, under the guidance of Arsaces (the family name of all their subsequent kings) they revolted from Antiochus Theus, the then king of Syria. It was not, however, until the year 230 B.C. that their empire became firmly established, when Arsaces defeated and took prisoner Seleucus Callicinus, the Syrian monarch, and first assumed the title of King of Parthia. By degrees they expelled the Syrian dominion from every province over which it extended east of the Euphrates; so that from about the year 140 B.C. their vast empire reached from the Ganges to the Euphrates, and from the Euphrates to the Caucasus." These facts would therefore lead to the conclusion that the Book of Enoch was written about the middle of the second century B.C.; but as the author adds to the passage already cited,

"They shall go up, and tread upon the land of their elect, the land of their elect shall be before them. The threshing-floor, the path, and the city of my righteous people shall impede the progress of their horses," Archbishop Laurence connects this language with the invasion of Syria by the Parthians in the year 54 B.C., and their defeat of Anthony eighteen years later, "when the credit of the Parthian arms was at the highest; and it is probable that about the same period, or at least not long after, the Book of Enoch was written."

The question now naturally arises, How was this work of fiction accepted within so short a period, as the genuine production of the patriarch Enoch? The Archbishop answers by showing, through internal evidence, that the book was written by a Jew residing at a distance from Palestine, and having been brought into Judæa in the name of the prophet Enoch, the obscurity of its origin caused some to accept it as the genuine production of the patriarch himself. In chapter lxxi. Pseudo-Enoch divides the day and night into eighteen parts, and represents the longest day in the year as consisting of twelve out of these eighteen parts. "Now the proportion of twelve to eighteen is precisely the same as sixteen to four and twenty, the present division in hours of the period constituting day and night. If therefore we consider in what latitude a country must be situated to have a day of sixteen hours long, we shall immediately perceive that Palestine could not be such a country. We may then safely conclude that the region in which the author lived must have been situated not lower than forty-five degrees north latitude, where the longest day is fifteen hours and a half, nor higher perhaps than forty- nine degrees, where the longest day is precisely sixteen hours. This will bring the country where he wrote, as high up at least as the northern districts of the Caspian and Euxine seas; probably it was situated somewhere between the upper parts of both these seas; and if the latter conjecture be well founded, the author of the Book of Enoch was perhaps a member of one of the tribes which Shalmaneser carried away, and placed 'in Halah and in Habor by the river Goshen, and in the cities of the Medes,' and who never returned from captivity."

Since Archbishop Laurence wrote his "Preliminary Dissertation," fresh light has been thrown on the origin of the Book of Enoch through the publication of Mr. Layard's "Nineveh and Babylon," recording the discovery, in Babylonian ruins, of cups or bowls of terra cotta, covered on the inner surface with inscriptions in ink, which have been deciphered by Mr. Thomas Ellis of the Manuscript Department in the British Museum, as amulets or charms against evil spirits, disease, calamity, and sudden death, composed in the Chaldean language mingled with Hebrew words,[7] and written in characters which combine Syriac and Palmyrene with the ancient Phoenician. These inscriptions are undated; but Mr. Ellis attained the conclusion through internal evidence, that these cups belonged to the descendants of the Jews who were carried captive to Babylon and the surrounding cities.

But the most important revelation attained through these discoveries of Mr. Layard lies in the interesting fact, mentioned in his work, that the names of the angels inscribed on these cups, and those recorded in the Book of Enoch, are, in many instances identical, so that no doubt remains as to the Hebrew-Chaldee origin of that great Semitic work, whether assignable to human genius or Divine revelation; and the exhumed amulets of Jews of the Dispersion attest the accuracy of Archbishop Laurence's conclusions respecting the nationality of Pseudo- Enoch.

Ignorance of the contents of the Apocrypha, as canonized by the Church of Rome, is so general in England that many otherwise well-informed people imagine that the Book of Enoch may be found in its pages, whereas it has been lost to all English readers, except those who may possess or have access to copies of the English translation last issued in 1838. On this aspect of the question Archbishop Laurence writes:—

"The fate of the Apocryphal writings in general has been singular. On one side, from the influence of theological opinion or theological caprice, they have been sometimes injudiciously admitted into the Canon of Scripture; while on the other side, from an over-anxiety to preserve that Canon inviolate, they have been not simply rejected, but loaded with every epithet of contempt and obloquy. The feelings perhaps of both parties have on such occasions run away with their judgment. For writings of this description, whatever may or may not be their claim to inspiration, are at least of considerable utility, where they indicate the theological opinions of the periods at which they were composed. This I

---

[7] "Halleluiah" appears upon the cups; and thus a word, with which ancient Syro-Chaldæans conjured, has become, through the vicissitudes of language, the Shibboleth of modern "Revivalists."

apprehend to be peculiarly the case of the Book of Enoch; which, as having been manifestly written before the doctrines of Christianity were promulgated to the world, must afford us, when it refers to the nature and character of the Messiah, as it repeatedly does so refer, credible proof of what were the Jewish opinions upon those points before the birth of Christ; and consequently before the possible predominance of the Christian creed."

Archbishop Laurence thus clearly recognized that the visions of Enoch preceded the teaching of Jesus; but it was not given to him, or to his generation, to see how deeply his conclusions affected the supernatural claims of Christianity.

Turning to the contents of the Book of Enoch, the first six chapters announce the condemnation of transgressors and the blessings of the righteous, through the triumphal advent of the Messiah, forecast in the famous prediction quoted by the author of the Epistle attributed to Jude.

Chapters vii. to xvi. record the descent of two hundred angels on the earth, their selection of wives, the birth of their gigantic offspring, and the instruction of mankind in the manufacture of offensive and defensive weapons, the fabrication of mirrors, the workmanship of jewellery, and the use of cosmetics and dyes, combined with lessons in sorcery, astrology, divination, and astronomy—all which Tertullian accepts as Divine revelation, when he denounces woman as the "devil's gateway,"[8] and assures her, on the authority of the inspired Enoch, that Tyrian dyes, Phrygian embroidery, Babylonian cloth, golden bracelets, gleaming pearls, flashing onyx-stones, and brilliant emeralds, with all the other adjuncts of an elegant toilette, are the special gifts of fallen angels to female frailty. The advent of the angels multiplies transgressions on earth, they are condemned to "the lowest depths of the fire in torments," and Enoch, as the messenger of God, announces to them the eternity of their punishment.

Chapters xvii. to xxxvi. give a graphic description of the miraculous journeys of Enoch in the company of an angel, from whom he learns the secrets of creation and the mysteries of Infinity. From the top of a lofty

[8] "On Female Dress," bk. i. chap. i.

mountain "which reached to heaven," he beheld the receptacles of light, thunder, and lightning, "the great darkness or mountains of gloom which constitute winter, the mouths of rivers and of the deep, the stone which supports the corners of the earth, and the four winds which bear up the earth, and constitute the pillars of heaven."[9] Is not this obviously the inspired cosmology, through which the author of the Book of Enoch unconsciously condemned mediæval physicists to the stake for impiously proclaiming the mobility of the earth? If an inspired prophet saw the stone which supports the corners of the earth, how inexpiable the guilt of men, who fostered scepticism through the heliocentric theory of a world coursing swiftly round the sun!

But had not the Book of Enoch disappeared for centuries out of Europe, before the persecution of Galileo and the martyrdom of Bruno? We answer that its teaching had survived, as numerous other superstitions have passed from generation to generation long after all knowledge of their origin has been lost to the theologians who accept them as Divine.

In the "Evolution of Christianity" we cite the following passage from Irenæus: "It is impossible that the Gospels can be more or less than they are. For as there are four zones in the world which we inhabit, and four principal winds, while the Church is spread abroad throughout the earth, and the pillar and basis of the Church is the gospel and the spirit of life, it is right that she should have four pillars exhaling immortality on every side, and bestowing renewed vitality on men. From which *fact* it follows that the Word has given us four versions of the Gospel, united by one spirit." We now recognize that this fanciful theory of a limited number of Evangelists is based on the cosmology of Enoch; and if in the second century, Irenæus accepted the visions of an antediluvian patriarch as facts, the traditional survival of the earth's "corner stone" doubtless controlled the orthodox astronomy of mediaeval theologians.

Proceeding on his journey with the angel Uriel, Enoch furthermore beheld the prison of the fallen angels, in which struggling columns of fire ascended from an appalling abyss. He saw the regions in which the spirits of the dead await the day of judgment; he looked upon the trees of knowledge and of life, exhaling fragrant odours from leaves which never withered, and from fruit which ever bloomed; and he beheld the "great

[9] Chap. xviii.

and glorious wonder" of the celestial stars, coming forth through the "gates of heaven."

Chapters xxxvii. to lxxi. record the second vision of wisdom, divided into three parables. The first depicts the future happiness and glory of the elect, whom Enoch beheld reclining on couches in the habitations of angels, or standing in thousands of thousands and myriads of myriads before the throne of God, blessing and glorifying Him with celestial song, as the Holy, Holy Lord of spirits, before whom righteousness eternally dwells.

As Enoch uttered his prophecies respecting the elect, before the existence of Christianity, it is important to learn in what sense he understood the doctrine of election. The language of the first parable happily leaves no room for doubt—"The righteous will be elected for their . good works duly weighed by the Lord of Spirits."[10] Election, therefore, traced to its original source, means nothing more than Divine "selection of the fittest"—a theory more consistent with the justice of God, than the capricious choice of the metamorphical potter, whose arbitrary fashioning of plastic clay symbolized, in Pauline theology, the doctrine of predestination.

The second parable (xlv.-lv.) demands the absorbed attention of modern Jews and Gentiles; for it is either the inspired forecast of a great Hebrew prophet, predicting with miraculous accuracy the future teaching of Jesus of Nazareth, or the Semitic romance from which the latter borrowed His conceptions of the triumphant return of the Son of man, to occupy a judicial throne in the midst of rejoicing saints and trembling sinners, expectant of everlasting happiness or eternal fire: and whether these celestial visions be accepted as human or Divine, they have exercised so vast an influence on the destinies of mankind for nearly two thousand years, that candid and impartial seekers after religious truth can no longer delay inquiry into the relationship of the Book of Enoch with the revelation, or the evolution, of Christianity.

The third parable (lvi.-lxx.) recurs, with glowing eloquence, to the inexhaustible theme of Messianic glory, and again depicts the happy future of the righteous in contrast with the appalling misery of the

---

[10] Chap. xxxviii. 2.

wicked. It also records the supernatural control. of the elements, through the action of individual angels presiding over the winds, the sea, hail, frost, dew, the lightning's flash, and reverberating thunder. The names of the principal fallen angels are also given, among whom we recognize some of the invisible powers named in the incantations inscribed on the terra cotta cups of Hebrew-Chaldee conjuration.

Chapters lxxi. to lxxxi. contain the "book of the revolutions of the luminaries of heaven," the sun, the moon, and the stars, controlled in their movements by the administration of angels. In commenting on this section of the Book of Enoch, Archbishop Laurence says, "This system of astronomy is precisely that of an untutored, but accurate observer of the heavens. He describes the eastern and western parts of heaven, where the sun and moon rise and set, as divided each into six different gates, through which those orbs of light pass at their respective periods. In the denomination of these gates he begins with that through which the sun passes at the winter solstice; and this he terms the *first* gate. It of course answers to the sign of Capricornus; and is the southernmost point to which the sun reaches, both at rising and setting. The next gate, at which the sun arrives in its progress towards the east at rising, and towards the west at setting, and which answers to the sign of Aquarius, he terms the *second* gate. The next, in continuation of the same course of the sun, which answers to the sign of Pisces, he terms the *third* gate.
The *fourth* gate in his description is that which is situated due east at sun-rising, and due west at sun-setting, and which, answering to the sign of Aries, the sun enters at the vernal equinox. With this *fourth* gate he commences his account of the sun's annual circuit, and of the consequent change in the length of day and night at the various seasons of the year. His *fifth* gate is now to be found in the sun's progress northwards, and answers to the sign of Taurus. And his *sixth* gate is situated still further north; which, answering to the sign of Gemini, concludes at the most northern point of heaven to which the sun arrives,
and from which it turns at the summer solstice, again to measure back its course southwards.

"Hence it happens, that the same gates which answers to the six signs alluded to in the sun's passage from the winter to the summer solstice, necessarily also answer to the remaining six of the twelve signs of the Zodiac in its passage back again.

"The turning of the sun both at the winter and summer solstices, the first at the most southern, the last at the most northern point of its progress, must have always struck the eye of those who contemplated the variety as well as the splendour of its daily appearance. The astronomy of the apocryphal Enoch was perhaps formed in this respect upon the same principles as the astronomy of Homer, who places the situation of the island Συρίη under the *turning of the sun*, ὅθι τροπαὶ ἠελίοιο (Odyss. lib. xv. 404)."

Chapters lxxxiii. to lxxxix. contain a vision of Enoch giving an allegorical forecast of the history of the world up to the kingdom of the Messiah.

Chapter xcii. records a series of prophecies extending from Enoch's own time to about one thousand years beyond the present generation. In the system of chronology adopted, a day stands for hundred, and a week for seven hundred years. Reference is made to the deluge, the call of Abraham, the Mosaic dispensation, the building and the destruction of the Temple of Solomon—events which preceded the date at which the Book of Enoch was probably written: but when the author, in his character of a divinely inspired seer, extends his vision beyond the horizon of his own age, he discloses the vanity of his predictive pretensions, through prophecies which remain unfulfilled. If, however, the Book of Enoch had reached us through the Western, as well as the Ethiopic Canon, apologetic theologians would doubtless affirm that centuries are but trifles in prophetic time; and that the predictions of the great antediluvian prophet shall, sooner or later, attain miraculous fulfilment.

Chapters xciii. to civ. contain the eloquent exhortations of Enoch, addressed to his children, in which he follows Buddha in commending the "Paths of Righteousness," and anticipates Jesus in pronouncing the doom of sinners and the joys of saints, and gives utterance to the most emphatic assurance of immortality which ever flowed from human lips: "Fear not, ye souls of the righteous, but wait with patient hope for the day of your death in righteousness. Grieve not because your souls descend in trouble and sorrow to the receptacle of the dead; for great joy shall be yours, like that of the angels in heaven. And when you die, sinners say concerning you, 'As we die the righteous die. What profit have they in their works? Behold, like us, they expire in sorrow and in darkness. What advantage have they over us? Henceforward are we equal; for behold they are dead, and never will they again perceive the light.' But now I swear to you, ye righteous . . . that I comprehend this mystery; that I have read the tablet of heaven, have seen the writing of the holy ones, and have discovered what is written and impressed on it concerning you. I have seen that all goodness, joy, and glory have been prepared for you.........The spirits of you who die in righteousness shall exist and rejoice; and their remembrance shall be before the face of the Mighty One from generation to generation.[11] How profound the impression necessarily produced on the Semitic imagination by this impassioned language, uttered in an age of faith in inspired dreams and celestial visions by a supposed visitant of the unseen world, who had conversed with angels in the presence of the Lord of spirits!

The final chapter of the Book of Enoch records the birth of Noah, and the further prophecies of Enoch, addressed to Methuselah on the subject of the birth of Noah and the future deluge.

In attestation of the relationship between the Book of Enoch and Christianity, we now collate its language and ideas with parallel passages in New Testament scripture.

En. lxiv. 4. "And a voice was heard from heaven."

Matt. iii. 17. "And lo, a voice from heaven, saying."

En. vi. 9. "The elect shall possess light, joy, and peace, and they shall inherit the earth."

Matt. v. 5. "Blessed are the meek, for they shall inherit the earth."

En. l. 2, 4, 5. "He shall select the righteous and holy from among them; for the day of their salvation has approached . . . and they shall become angels in heaven. Their countenances shall

Luke xxi. 28. " Your redemption draweth nigh."
Matt. xxii. 30. "In the resurrection . . . they are as the angels of God in heaven."
Matt. xiii. 43. "Then shall the righteous shine

---

[11] Chap. cii., ciii.

be bright with joy........ The earth shall rejoice; and the elect possess it."

forth as the sun in the kingdom of their Father."

En. xciii. 7. "Those, too, who acquire gold and silver, shall justly and suddenly perish. Woe to you who are rich, for in your riches have you trusted; but from your riches you shall be removed."

James v. 1. "Go to now, ye rich men, weep and howl for your miseries that shall come upon you."

Luke vi. 24. "Woe unto you that are rich! for ye have received your consolation."

En. xcvi. 6, 7, 25. "Woe unto you, sinners, who say, 'We are rich, possess wealth, and have acquired everything which we can desire. Now then will we do whatsoever we are disposed to do; for we have amassed silver; our barns are full.' . . . They shall surely die suddenly."

Luke xii. Compare the parable of the rich man whose barns were full, and who said to himself, "Soul, thou hast much goods laid up for many years, take thine ease, eat, drink, and be merry. But God said unto him, Thou fool, this night thy soul shall be required of thee."

En. cv. 26. "And I will place each of them on a throne of glory, of glory peculiarly his own."

Matt. xix. 28. "Ye also shall sit upon twelve thrones, judging the twelve tribes of Israel."

En. lxii. 11. "In his judgments he pays no respect to persons."

Rom. ii. 11. "For there is no respect of persons with God."

En. xxxviii. 2. "Where will the habitation of sinners be . . . who have rejected the Lord of spirits. It would have been better for them, had they never been born."

Matt. xxvi. 24. "Woe unto that man through whom the Son of man is betrayed! It would be good for that man if he had not been born."

En. xix. 2. "So that they sacrifice to devils as to Gods."

1 Cor. x. 20. "The things which the Gentiles sacrifice, they sacrifice to devils, and not to God."

En. xxii. 10, 12. (The angel Raphael addressing Enoch in the region of the dead:) "Here their souls are separated . . . by a chasm."

Luke xvi. 26 (Abraham addressing Dives from the region of the blessed:) "Between us and you there is a great gulf fixed."

En. xxxix. 3, 4, 7. "A cloud then snatched me up . . . placing me at the extremity of the heavens. There I saw another vision. I saw the habitations and couches of the saints . . . with the angels . . . under the wings of the Lord of spirits. All the holy and the elect sung before him, in appearance like a blaze of fire, their mouths being full of blessings, and their lips glorifying the name of the Lord of spirits."

2 Cor. xii. "I will come to visions and revelations of the Lord. I knew a man in Christ . . . caught up to the third heaven, . . . whether in the body or out of the body I cannot tell: God knoweth. How that he was caught up into paradise, and heard unspeakable words, which it is not lawful for a man to utter."

Rev. xix. 1. "I heard a great voice of much people in heaven, saying, Alleluia, salvation, and glory, and honour, and power, unto the Lord our God."

En. xlvi. 2. "This is the Son of man . . . who will reveal all the treasures of that which is concealed."

Col. ii. 3. "In whom are hid all the treasures of wisdom and knowledge."

En. ix. 3, 4. "Then they said to their Lord, the King: Thou art Lord of lords, God of gods, King of kings. The

Rev. xvii. 14; xix. 16. "King of kings, and Lord of lords."

Rev. iv. 11. "Thou art

throne of thy glory is for ever and ever, and for ever and ever is thy name sanctified and glorified. Thou art blessed and glorified. Thou hast made all things; thou possessest power over all things: and all things are open and manifest before thee. Thou beholdest all things, and nothing can be concealed from thee."

worthy O Lord, to receive glory, and honour, and power; for thou hast created all things, and for thy pleasure they are, and were created."

Heb. iv. 13. " Neither is there any creature that is not manifest in his sight; but all things are naked and opened unto the eyes of him with whom we have to do."

En. xxiv. 11, 10, "I blessed the Lord of glory, the everlasting King, because He has prepared this tree for the saints, formed it, and declared that he would give it to them .... The sweet odour shall enter into their bones; and they shall live a long life on the earth, as thy forefathers have lived; neither in their days shall sorrow, distress, and punishment afflict them."

Rev. xxii. 2. "On either side of the river was a tree of life, which bare twelve manner of fruits, and yielded its fruit every month; and the leaves of the tree were for the healing of the nations."

Rev. ii. 7. "To him that overcometh will I give to eat of the tree of life, which is in the midst of the paradise of God."

Rev. xxii. 14. "Blessed are they that do his commandments, that they may have the right to the tree of life."

En. lxxxv. 2. "And behold a single star fell from heaven."

Rev. ix. 1. "I saw a star fall from heaven unto the earth."

En. lx. 13. "All the angels of power."

2 Thess. i. "The angels of His power."

En. x. 15, 16. "To Michael

Jude 6. "The angels which

also, the Lord said, Go and announce his crime to Samyaza and to the others who are with him who have been associated with women........Bind them for seventy generations underneath the earth, even to the day of judgment, and of consummation, until the judgment, which shall last for ever, be completed. Then shall they be taken away into the lowest depths of the fire in torments, and in confinement shall they be shut up for ever."

kept not their first estate, but left their own habitation, he hath reserved in everlasting chains under darkness, unto the judgment of the great day."

2 Pet. ii. 4. "God spared not the angels when they sinned, but cast them down to hell, and committed them to pits of darkness, to be reserved unto judgment."

Rev. xx. 10. "The devil that deceived them was cast into the lake of fire and brimstone, . . . and shall be tormented day and night for ever."

En. xxi. 56. "I beheld columns of fire struggling together to the end of the abyss, and deep was their

Rev. xx. 1-3. "And I saw an angel come down from heaven, having the key of the bottomless pit

descent. But neither its measurement nor magnitude was I able to discover .... Uriel, one of the holy angels.......said, This is the prison of the angels, and here are they kept for ever."

(abyss) and a great chain in his hand. And he laid hold on the devil and . . . cast him into the bottomless pit, and shut it, and sealed it over him."

En. lxxix. "In the days of sinners the years shall be shortened, . . . and every thing done on earth shall be subverted and disappear in its season........In those days

Matt. xxiv. 7, 21, 22, 29, 30. " There shall be famines and earthquakes in divers places . . . great tribulation, such as was not since the beginning of the world to this time, no,

the fruits of the earth shall not flourish in their season, . . . heaven shall stand still. The moon shall change its laws, and not be seen at its proper period; . . . and all the classes of the stars shall be shut up against sinners."

En. lxi. 9. "And trouble shall seize them when they shall behold this Son of woman sitting upon the throne of his glory."

nor ever shall be. And except those days should be shortened, there should no flesh be saved. . . . Immediately after the tribulation of those days, the sun shall be darkened, and the moon shall not give her light, and the stars shall fall from heaven............... Then shall the tribes of the earth mourn; and they shall see the Son of man coming in the clouds of heaven, with power and great glory."

En. xlvii. 3. "He sat upon the throne of his glory, while the book of the living was opened in his presence, and while all the powers which were above the heavens stood around and before him."

En. l. "In those days shall the

Rev. xx. 11-13,15. "I saw a great white throne, and him that sat on it, . . . and I saw the dead, small and great, standing before the throne; and the books were opened, and another book was opened, which is the book of life, and the dead were judged out of

earth deliver up from her womb, and hell deliver up from hers, that which it has received, and destruction shall restore that which it owes. He shall select the righteous and holy from among them."

En. liv. "In those days shall the mouth of hell be opened into which they shall he immerged; hell shall destroy

and swallow up sinners from the face of the elect."

those things what were written in the books, according to their works. And the sea gave up the dead which were in it, and death and hell delivered up the dead which were in them..............................And whosoever was not found written in the book of life was cast into the lake of fire.

En. xl. 1. "After this I beheld thousands of thousands, and ten thousand times ten thousand, and an infinite number of people, standing before the Lord of spirits."

Rev. v. 11. "I beheld, and I heard the voice of many angels round about the throne, . . . and the number of them was ten thousand times ten thousand, and thousands of thousands."

En. xlv. 3. "In that day shall the Elect One sit upon a throne of glory, and shall choose their conditions and countless habitations."

Matt. xxv. 31, 32. "Then shall he sit upon the throne of his glory; and before him shall be gathered all nations; and he shall separate them one from another."

John xiv. 2. " In my father's house are many habitations."

En. xlv. 4. "In that day I will cause my Elect One to dwell in the

Rev. vii. 15. "He that sitteth on the throne shall dwell among them."

midst of them. I will change the face of the heaven: I will bless it and illuminate it for ever. I will also change the face of the earth: I will bless it, and cause those whom I have chosen to dwell upon it."

2 Peter iii. 13. "Nevertheless, we, according to his promise, look for new heavens and a new earth, wherein dwelleth righteousness."

En. xcii. 17. "The former heaven shall depart and pass away, a new heaven shall appear."

Rev. xxii. 1. "I saw a new heaven and a new earth, for the first heaven and the first earth were passed away."

En. lxi. 4-9. "The word of his mouth shall destroy all sinners, and all the ungodly

who shall perish at his presence. . . . Trouble shall come upon them, as upon a woman in travail. One portion of them shall look upon another; they shall be astonished, and shall abase their countenances; and trouble shall seize them, when they shall behold this Son of woman sitting upon the throne of His glory."

2 Thess. i. 9. "Who shall be punished with everlasting destruction from the presence

of the Lord, and from the glory of his power."

1 Thess. v. 3. "Then sudden destruction cometh upon them as travail upon a woman with child, and they shall not escape."

2 Thess. ii. 8. "That wicked whom the Lord shall consume with the Spirit of his mouth."

Matt. xxv. 31. "When the Son of man shall come in his glory, then shall he sit upon the throne of his glory."

En. lxvi. 5-8. "I beheld that valley in which . . . arose a strong smell of sulphur which became mixed with the waters; and the valley of the angels, who had been guilty of seduction, burned underneath its soil. Through that valley also rivers of fire were flowing, to which the angels shall be condemned, who seduced the inhabitants of the earth."

Matt. xiii. 42. "And shall cast them into a furnace of fire."

Matt. xxv. 41. "Depart from me, ye cursed, into everlasting fire, prepared for the devil and his angels."

Rev. xx. 10. "And the devil that deceived them was cast into the lake of fire and brimstone."

En. civ. "Now will I point out a mystery. Many sinners shall turn and transgress against the word of uprightness. They shall speak evil things; they shall utter falsehood."

1 Tim. iv. 12. "The Spirit saith expressly, that in later times some shall fall away from the faith, . . . through the hypocrisy of men that speak lies."

En. xlviii. 1-7. "In that place I beheld a fountain of righteousness which never failed, encircled by many springs of wisdom. Of these all the thirsty drank, and were filled with wisdom, having their habitation with the righteous, the elect, and the holy."

John iv. 14. "But whosoever drinketh of the water that I shall give him shall never thirst: but the water that I shall give him shall be in him a well of water springing up into everlasting life."

Rev. xxi. 6. "I will give unto him that is athirst of the fountain of the water of life freely."

En. xlviii. "He has preserved the lot of the righteous, because they have hated and rejected this world of iniquity, and have detested all its works and ways in the name of the Lord of spirits."

Gal. i. 4. "Who gave himself for our sins, that he might deliver us from this present evil world, according to the will of God and our Father."

1 John ii. 15. "Love not the world,

neither the things that are in the world."

En. ii. xxvi. 2. "Behold, he comes with ten thousands of his saints, to execute judgment upon them, and destroy the wicked, and reprove all the carnal for everything which the sinful and ungodly have done and committed against him .... [who utter with their mouths unbecoming language against God, and speak harsh things of his glory]."

Jude 14, 15. "Enoch also, the seventh from Adam, prophesied of these, saying, 'Behold, the Lord cometh with ten thousands of his saints, to execute judgment upon all, and to convict all the ungodly of all their ungodly deeds which they have ungodly committed, and of all the hard things which ungodly sinners have spoken against him."

The bracketed words, in the last quotation from the Book of Enoch, establish its complete identity with the parallel passage in the Epistle of Jude—an identity of marvellous clearness when we consider that the original version reaches us through translations and retranslations from Aramæan, Greek, and Ethiopic, and now assumes the modern form of Anglo-Saxon. Archbishop Laurence, although convinced that the apostle cited the Greek version of the extant Ethiopic manuscripts, was not aware that the last sentence of his quotation is present in the text. We have discovered it in chapter xxvi. 2 of the Book of Enoch; and in thus perfecting the parallelism between prophet and apostle, have placed beyond controversy that, in the eyes of the author of an Epistle accepted as Divine revelation, the Book of Enoch was the inspired production of an antediluvian patriarch.

The attention of theologians has been concentrated on the passage in the Epistle of Jude because the author specifically names the prophet; but the cumulative coincidence of language and ideas in Enoch and the authors of New Testament Scripture, as disclosed in the parallel passages which we have collated, clearly indicates that the work of the Semitic Milton was the inexhaustible source from which Evangelists and Apostles, or the men who wrote in their names, borrowed their conceptions of the resurrection, judgment, immortality, perdition, and of the universal reign of righteousness under the eternal dominion of the Son of man. This evangelical plagiarism culminates in the Revelation of John, which adapts the visions of Enoch to Christianity with modifications in which we miss the sublime simplicity of the great master of apocalyptic prediction, who prophesied in the name of the antediluvian patriarch.

It is important to observe that it was not the practice of early Christian writers to name the authors whose language and ideas they borrowed. When we therefore detect the teaching and diction of Enoch in Gospels and Epistles, our conclusions are analogous to those of the orthodox theologians who identify passages of Scripture in the pages of the ante-Nicene Fathers, although frequently cited from unnamed sources, with an obscurity of expression more dubious in attestation of their origin, than the remarkable clearness with which the language of Enoch may be recognized in the New Testament. Biblical analysts may question obscure traces of evangelical diction in apostolic Fathers; but what candid and impartial inquirer can doubt the Enochian origin of the "Son of man sitting upon the throne of his glory"—the "new heaven" and the "new earth;" the "many habitations" of the elect, and "the everlasting fire prepared for the devil and his angels "?

We have merely collated some of the most striking instances of parallel passages in the Book of Enoch and in the New Testament. Our readers can supplement our labours through their own research, in further attestation of the controlling influence exercised by the uncanonical author on the language and ideas of canonical works.

Some orthodox theologians, unwilling to admit that an apostle quoted an apocryphal book, contend that Jude referred to a traditional utterance of the ancient patriarch; but this obviously fanciful theory inevitably vanishes in the presence of the numerous passages from the Book of Enoch, which enter into the composition of New Testament Scripture. Other pious apologists affirm the post-Christian authorship of the book, a theory which involves the most improbable assumption that an author, familiar with the story of a suffering and crucified Messiah, uttered fictitious predictions in the name of an ancient prophet, which depicted the career of the Son of man on earth as the triumphal march of a victorious king. Again, theologians who shrink from the admission that the language and ideas of evangelists and apostles were anticipated in an apocryphal book, suggest that the Messianic passages contain Christian interpolations. But if modern defenders of the faith thus accuse primitive saints and martyrs of literary forgery, how can they accept an infallible New Testament at the hands of men thus guilty of conspiring for the deception of posterity? Convinced of the honesty of early Christians, we concur with the opinion of Archbishop Laurence, confirmed by Hoffman, that the passages in question are so intimately interwoven with the general context that they cannot be removed without evidently destroying the texture of the whole.

The astronomical calculations on which Archbishop Laurence based his theory of the residence of the author of the Book of Enoch have been questioned; but, once his Hebrew nationality has been admitted, it matters not whether he wrote in or out of Palestine, with this exception, that if the work was not brought from a distant country into Judaea, the facility with which a pseudonymous book was accepted in the locality of its recent composition as the genuine production of an antediluvian prophet, necessarily encourages scepticism as to the dates and authorship of all ancient Hebrew literature. It cannot be said that internal evidence attests the superiority of the Old Testament to the Book of Enoch; for no Hebrew prophet is more eloquent than its author in denouncing iniquity, commending righteousness, and inviting all men to place implicit trust in the final vindication of Divine justice.

Internal evidence indicates the presence of independent Tracts in the Book of Enoch, possibly composed by different authors. Thus chapters lxiv. to lxvii.[12] record a vision of the Deluge, narrated as if by Noah instead of Enoch, and inserted in the middle of another vision with which it has no connection. But if Pseudo-Enoch borrowed from earlier writers, the presence of the language and ideas of every section of his work in the pages of New Testament Scripture inevitably indicates that the Book or Books of Enoch existed in their present form before the Christian era.

---

[12] In "The Evolution of Christianity," page 355, we mention that "the Greek word αἰών (æon), signifying an age, a generation, or time everlasting," was the title adopted by Valentinus for Divine emanations.

Christianity obviously borrows the terrors of eternal fire from the Book of Enoch. Evangelists and Apostles define the duration of Divine retribution by æons of æons 1 (αἱ αἰῶνες τῶν αἰώνων), or millions of millions of years, expressive of eternity. It is true that the word æon can be used in the sense of finite time, but when the authors of New Testament Scripture speak of æonian fire (τὸ πῦρ τὸ αἰώνιον) they obviously mean eternal flames. Modern humanity, shrinking from so merciless a view of Divine retribution, suggests that when sinners have been tortured for æons of æons they may look forward hopefully to the future. It is questionable whether final despair would not be preferable to this form of "hope deferred;" but if modern believers adopt the terminable theory of æonian fire, this commutation of sentence becomes equally applicable to the devil and his angels, whose punishment has been decreed of same duration as that of human sinners;[13] and thus the traditional enemies of God and man may hope for joyful restoration to fellowship with Gabriel, Michael, and Raphael, and communion with the saints, whom they once sought to betray by arts infernal. And as the righteous are also only promised their rewards in heaven for æons of æons,[14] if these words mean not eternity, saints may fear, whilst sinners hope for, the vicissitudes of æonian futurity. Again, as the dominion of the Messiah,[15] and even the power of God,[16] are depicted of æonian duration, any limitation of the infinite in the sacred terminology—æons of æons—imperils the eternal in Divinity.

Theologians who seek to vindicate Divine clemency through the dubious expedient of substituting æonian for eternal retribution, overlook the fact that their theory imputes to Divine wisdom the adoption of torture as the most effectual means of transforming sinners into saints,—a theory which practically invites us to follow the Divine example by torturing our criminals into reformation. How much more consistent for those who cannot reconcile eternal fire with infinite mercy, to take one step further in the paths of scepticism, by rejecting everlasting torture as the nightmare of Enochian visions; instead of assuming that revelation speaks in language so ambiguous that primitive saints condemned unbaptized babes to eternal fire, whilst modern piety would even rescue

[13] Matt. xxv. 41; Rev. xx. 10.
[14] Rev. xxii. 5.
[15] Rev. xi. 15.
[16] Rev. vii. 12.

hardened sinners from the flames! If inspired terminology encouraged spiritual ferocity in the age of St. Augustine, and fosters theological humanity in the nineteenth century, what may not be the future interpretation of words, now supposed to convey an infallible meaning to students of Scripture?

The Book of Enoch teaches the pre-existence of the Son of Man, the Elect One, the Messiah, who "from the beginning existed in secret,"[17] and whose "name was invoked in the presence of the Lord of spirits, before the sun and the signs were created."[18] The author also refers to the "other Power who was upon earth over the water on that day,"[19] —an apparent reference to the language of Gen. i. 2. We have thus the Lord of spirits, the Elect One, and a third Power, seemingly foreshadowing the Trinity of futurity; but although Enoch's ideal Messiah doubtless exercised an important influence on primitive conceptions of the Divinity of the Son of man, we fail to identify his obscure reference to another "Power" with the Trinitarianism of the Alexandrine school; more especially as "angels of power" abound in the visions of Enoch.

That remarkable passage in the Book of Enoch, which declares that the heathen "sacrificed to devils as to gods,"[20] is the obvious source of that superstition through which primitive Christianity saw in Olympian deities, not the mere phantoms of man's imagination, but the fallen angels who, driven forth from heaven, sought compensation in spiritual dominion on earth,—a superstition still further confirmed by universal belief in miracles, wrought, not merely by the Supreme, but by subordinate powers, whether good or evil.

Thus far we learn that the Book of Enoch was published before the Christian era by some great Unknown of Semitic race, who, believing himself to be inspired in a post-prophetic age, borrowed the name of an antediluvian patriarch to authenticate his own enthusiastic forecast of the Messianic kingdom. And as the contents of his marvellous Book enter freely into the composition of the New Testament, it follows that if the author was not an inspired prophet, who predicted the teaching of Christianity, he was a visionary enthusiast whose illusions were accepted

[17] Chap. lxi. 10.
[18] Chap. xlviii.
[19] Chap. lx.
[20] Chap. xix. 2.

by Evangelists and Apostles as revelation—alternative conclusions which involve the Divine or human origin of Christianity.

It may be said that if the author of the Book of Enoch was not the patriarch in whose name he wrote, was he not obviously an impostor? In treating of Hebrew divination in "The Evolution of Christianity," we refer to the oracles of Urim and the predictions of Prophets. There was, however, a third form of divination, known as Bath Kol, or the Daughter of the Voice, through which the Israelites consulted the Deity by accepting some preconceived sign in attestation of the Divine approval of contemplated action. This method of artificial (τεχνικη?<I?>?) divination is said to have succeeded the revelation of prophets, but was practised by the Israelites at a much earlier period of their history. Thus the servant of Abraham predetermined the sign through which he would recognize the future wife of Isaac as divinely chosen; and Jonathan, the son of Saul, preconcerted the verbal omen through which the Israelites might know that Jehovah had delivered the Philistines into their hands.

The practice of Bath Kol was doubtless familiar to the Semitic author of the Book of Enoch; let us not therefore condemn him as an impostor, knowing that through the accidental synchronism of some pre-arranged sign, he may have personated Enoch in the conscientious conviction that he was piously fulfilling the will of the Deity.

The recent death of Dr. Pusey recalls the fact, that the learned translator of the Book of Enoch was his predecessor as Professor of Hebrew in the University of Oxford. The friends and admirers of the eminent theologian, who was one of the authors of the Tractarian movement, propose to found a memorial Library in his name, with "two or more clergymen, who shall act as librarians, and shall promote *in whatever way* the interests of theological study and religious life within the University"—a programme which seems to inaugurate the reign of original research within the domains of ecclesiastical theology. But if, as we are informed by the promoters of the proposed endowment, Dr. Pusey was above all things "a Christian apologist, the advocate and champion of the Church of eighteen centuries," how can the disciples, who saw in him the "great pillar which once sustained the fortunes of the Church of England," encourage a freedom of inquiry, in his name, which may result in conclusions adverse to the ecclesiastical faith in which their master lived and died?

Eminent theologians tell us that the future librarians "should be students of theology—the queen of sciences,—among whom Dr. Pusey held a position in the first rank;" and yet that he was a zealous supporter of "a movement which embodied truths included ages ago in the formularies of the Church." But how can theology be enrolled among the sciences if its professors reason in ecclesiastical fetters? As well might a modern astronomer demand the assent of his pupils to the mediæval theory of the earth's immobility, before proceeding to investigate the laws of the solar system: and thus, doubtless, most theologians seek Divine truth, weighted with a heritage of foregone conclusions, adverse to the admission of unorthodox facts.

We all can sympathize with the desire of his disciples to do honour to the memory of the Tractarian apostle, of many virtues, in whom they see a "great man, raised up by God Almighty to live and labour for His Church;" but men who take this transcendental view of a movement, in which others simply see progress on the road to Rome, can scarcely consider the prescriptive rights of primitive or mediæval dogmas, in that impartial mood to which theologians must attain before theology becomes the "Queen of Sciences."

Archbishop Laurence was an industrious worker in the scientific laboratory of theology, when he translated the Bodleian manuscript of the Book of Enoch, and thus unconsciously placed in our hands the Ethiopic key to "the evolution of Christianity." It remains for future generations to determine whether his labours, or those of his successor in the Semitic chair of Oxford, shall prove more conducive to the religious enlightenment of posterity.

Palæontologists who compare the organic fossils of distinctive epochs in geologic time, and discover in the more recent formations, organisms partially divergent in structure from pre-existent forms, attribute variation, not to creative miracles, but to the continuous action of natural causes fashioning species, throughout the ages, in harmony with the natural law of " Survival of the Fittest." We also, having identified the kindred fossils of Enochian and Evangelical epochs, inevitably infer that modified versions of pre-existent ideas are traceable, not to miraculous, but to natural sources,—conclusions which inaugurate the science of theologic palæontology, and invite all learned travellers to follow the example of Bruce, by searching the world for ancient manuscripts which may disclose the merely human origin of dogmas and mysteries, now accepted as Divine.

Archbishop Laurence, when Professor of Hebrew in the University of Oxford, translated the Book of Enoch within the walls of the Bodleian Library, and when appealed to by the Rev. I. M. Butt, in 1827, to publish the Ethiopic original, answered, "I cannot, the manuscript not being my own, but belonging to the University of Oxford." In his preface to the third edition of his translation, the Archbishop adds, "If the University of Oxford would oblige the literary world by publishing the original Ethiopic from the manuscript in its possession, I am persuaded that Ethiopic scholars would not be wanting to accomplish more than has been hitherto done for this long regretted book, after its sleep of ages." Since these words were written, great progress has been made in the study of comparative philology; and there are now doubtless many eminent linguists in England, on the Continent, and in the United States, who could still further illumine the pages of the Book of Enoch, through co-operative criticism of the Ethiopic text. Is not the time therefore come for the University of Oxford to publish the original manuscript in their possession, that learned Jews and Gentiles may study the inspired predictions of a great Hebrew prophet, or admire the sublime imagery of the Semitic Milton who ascended to the heavens to dramatize Divinity?

At the era of the Renaissance, when enfranchised thought turned from Aristotle to Plato, it is said that Cardinal Bellarmine advised Pope Clement VIII. to discountenance a philosophy which approached so closely to the truths of the gospel—obviously meaning that it would be inexpedient for the Church to favour a merely human system which anticipated the Trinitarian theosophy of alleged revelation: is it not possible that further delay in presenting the world with the Ethiopic text of Enoch, may suggest to adverse critics, that Oxford neglects the Hebrew patriarch for the same reason that Rome slighted the Athenian philosopher?

Archbishop Laurence's translation, now however, places the Book of Enoch within the reach of all English readers. Catholics may disregard its contents, as it is not found in the sacred Canon of their infallible Church; but Protestants, who adhere to the principles of the Reformation, and whose tenure of Christianity is therefore contingent on the appeal to reason, must inevitably enroll Enoch among the prophets, or reconsider the supernatural in Christianity.

It is important for readers of the Book of Enoch to recollect that we owe the Reformation to independent study of sacred literature, previously withdrawn from the people through the oblivion of dead and untranslated languages. The long neglected Book of Enoch now stands in analogous relationship with modern seekers after religious truth; and it remains for its readers to exercise that right of private judgment, to which Protestantism owes its existence, by impartially considering the inevitable modifications of faith involved in the discovery, that the language and ideas of alleged revelation are found in a pre-existent work, accepted by Evangelists and Apostles as inspired, but classed by modern theologians among apocryphal productions.

[In revising the proof-sheets of the Book of Enoch, we have been still further impressed by its relationship with New Testament Scripture. Thus, the parable of the sheep, rescued by the good Shepherd from hireling guardians and ferocious wolves, is obviously borrowed by the fourth Evangelist from Enoch lxxxix}., in which the author depicts the shepherds as killing and destroying the sheep before the advent of their Lord, and thus discloses the true meaning of that hitherto mysterious passage in the Johannine parable—"All that ever came before me are thieves and robbers"—language in which we now detect an obvious reference to the allegorical shepherds of Enoch.]

CHAPTERS I-XX

CHAP I.

1. THE word of the blessing of Enoch, how he blessed the elect and the righteous, who were to exist in the time of trouble; rejecting[21] all the wicked and ungodly. Enoch, a righteous man, who was with God, answered and spoke, *while* his eyes were open, and while he saw a holy vision in the heavens.[22] This the angels showed me.

2. From them I heard all things, and understood what I saw; that which will not take place in this generation, but in a generation which is to succeed at a distant period, on account of the elect.

3. Upon their account I spoke and conversed with him, who will go forth from his habitation, the Holy and Mighty One, the God of the world:

4. Who will hereafter tread upon Mount Sinai; appear with his hosts; and be manifested in the strength of his power from heaven.

5. All shall be afraid, and the Watchers be terrified.

6. Great fear and trembling shall seize them, even to the ends of the earth. The lofty mountains shall be troubled, and the exalted hills depressed, melting like a honeycomb in the flame. The earth shall be immerged, and all things which are in it perish; while judgment shall come upon all, even upon all the righteous:

7. But to them shall he give peace: he shall preserve the elect, and towards them exercise clemency.

8. Then shall all belong to God; be happy and blessed; and the splendour of the Godhead shall illuminate them.

---

[21] *to the rejection of*. N.B. The Italic words in the text supply an ellipsis. In the notes they are used to mark the literal sense.
[22] *which* was *in the heavens.*

CHAP. II.

Behold, he comes with ten thousands of his saints, to execute judgment upon them, and destroy the wicked, and reprove all the carnal[23] for everything which the sinful and ungodly have done, and committed against him.[24]

CHAP. III.

1. All who are in the heavens know what is transacted[25] there.

2. They know that the heavenly luminaries change not their paths; that each rises and sets regularly, every one at its proper period, without transgressing the commands which they have received. They behold the earth, and understand what is there transacted, from the beginning to the end of it.

3. They see that every work of God is invariable in the period of its appearance. They behold summer and winter: perceiving that the whole earth is full of water; and that the cloud, the dew, and the rain refresh it.

CHAP. IV.

They consider and behold every tree, how it appears to wither, and every leaf to fall off, except of fourteen trees, which are not deciduous; which wait from the old, to the appearance of the new leaf, for two or three winters.

CHAP. V.

Again they consider the days of summer, that the sun is upon it at its very beginning; while you seek for a covered and shady spot on account of the burning sun; while the earth is scorched up with fervid heat, and

[23] of flesh.
[24] Quoted by St. Jude ver. 14, 15.
[25] *the work.*

you become incapable of walking either upon the ground or upon the rocks in consequence of that heat.

CHAP. VI.

1. They consider how the trees, when they put forth their green leaves, become covered, and produce fruit; understanding everything, and knowing that He who lives for ever does all these things for you:

2. *That* the works at the beginning of every existing year, that all his works, are subservient to him, and invariable; yet as God has appointed, so are all things brought to pass.

3. They see, too, how the seas and the rivers together complete their respective operations:

4. *But* you endure not patiently, nor fulfil the commandments of the Lord; but you transgress and calumniate *his* greatness; and malignant are the words in your polluted mouths against his Majesty.

5. Ye withered in heart, no peace shall be to you!

6. Therefore your days shall you curse, and the years of your lives shall perish; perpetual execration shall be multiplied, and you shall not obtain mercy.

7. In those days shall you resign your peace with the eternal maledictions of all the righteous, and sinners shall perpetually execrate you;

8. *Shall execrate* you with the ungodly.

9. The elect shall possess light, joy, and peace; and they shall inherit the earth.

10. But you, ye unholy, shall be accursed.

11. Then shall wisdom be given to the elect, all of whom shall live, and not again transgress by impiety or pride; but shall humble themselves, possessing prudence, and shall not repeat transgression.

12.   They shall not be condemned the whole period of their lives, nor die in torment and indignation; but the sum of their days[26] shall be completed, and they shall grow old in peace; while the years of their happiness shall be multiplied with joy, and with peace, for ever, the whole duration of their existence.

CHAP. VII. [SECT. II.[27]]

1.[28] It happened after the sons of men had multiplied in those days, that daughters were born to them, elegant and beautiful.

2. And when the angels, the sons of heaven, beheld them, they became enamoured of them, saying to each other, Come, let us select for ourselves wives from the progeny of men, and let us beget children.

3. Then their leader Samyaza said to them; I fear that you may perhaps be indisposed to the performance of this enterprise;

4. And that I alone shall suffer for so grievous a crime.

5. But they answered him and said; We all swear;

6. And bind ourselves by mutual execrations, that we will not change our intention, but execute our projected undertaking.

7. Then they swore all together, and all bound themselves by mutual execrations. Their whole number was two hundred, who descended upon Ardis, which is the top of mount Armon.

8. That mountain therefore was called[29] Armon, because they had sworn upon it, and bound themselves by mutual execrations.

9. These are the names of their chiefs: Samyaza, who was their leader, Urakabarameel, Akibeel, Tamiel, Ramuel, Danel, Azkeel, Saraknyal, Asael, Armers, Batraal, Anane, Zavebe, Samsaveel, Ertael, Turel, Yomyael, Arazyal. These were the prefects of the two hundred angels, and the remainder were all with them.

---

[26] *the days of their life.*
[27] Section II. Paris MS. transcribed by Woide.
[28] The first two extracts made by Syncellus from the Greek commence here, and end with the 15th verse of chap. x.
[29] *they called.*

10.   Then they took wives, each choosing for himself; whom they began to approach, and with whom they cohabited; teaching them sorcery, incantations, and the dividing of roots and trees.

11. [30] And the women[31] conceiving brought forth giants,

12.   Whose stature was each three hundred cubits. These devoured all which the labour of men produced; until it became impossible to feed them;

13. When they turned themselves against men, in order to devour them;

14.   And began to injure birds, beasts, reptiles, and fishes, to eat their flesh one after another, and to drink their blood.

15. Then the earth reproved the unrighteous.

CHAP. VIII.

1. Moreover Azazyel taught men to make swords, knives, shields, breastplates, the fabrication of mirrors,[32] and the workmanship of bracelets and ornaments, the use of paint, the beautifying of the eyebrows, *the use of* stones of every valuable and select kind, and of all sorts of dyes, so that the world became altered.

2. Impiety increased; fornication multiplied; and they transgressed and corrupted all their ways.

3. Amazarak taught all the sorcerers, and dividers of roots:

4. Armers *taught* the solution of sorcery;

5. Barkayal *taught* the observers of the stars;

6. Akibeel *taught* signs;

7. Tamiel *taught* astronomy;

8. And Asaradel taught the motion of the moon.

---

[30] This and the following verses of this chapter, viz. 11, 12, 13, 14, 15, seem to belong to the next chapter, and should perhaps be inserted between the 8th and 9th verses of that chapter. Such appears to be their situation in the Greek fragment, quoted by Syncellus.
[31] *They.*
[32] *made them see that which was behind them.*

9. And men, being destroyed, cried out; and their voice reached to heaven.

CHAP. IX.

1. Then Michael and Gabriel, Raphael, Suryal, and Uriel, looked down from heaven, and saw the quantity of blood which was shed on earth, and all the iniquity which was done upon it, and said one to another, *It is* the voice of their cries;

2. The earth deprived *of her children* has cried even to the gate of heaven.

3. And now to you, O ye holy ones of heaven, the souls of men complain, saying, Obtain Justice for us with[33] the Most High. Then they said to their Lord, the King, *Thou art* Lord of lords, God of gods, King of kings. The throne of thy glory is for ever and ever, and for ever and ever is thy name sanctified and glorified. Thou art blessed and glorified.

4. Thou hast made all things; thou possessest power over all things; and all things are open and manifest before thee. Thou beholdest all things, and nothing, can be concealed from thee.

5. Thou hast seen what Azazyel has done, how he as taught every species of iniquity upon earth, and has disclosed to the world all the secret things which are done in the heavens.

6. Samyaza also has taught sorcery, to whom thou hast given authority over those who are associated with him. They have gone together to the daughters of men; have lain with them; have become polluted;

7. And have discovered crimes to them.

8. The women likewise have brought forth giants.

9. Thus has the whole earth been filled with blood and with iniquity.

10. And now behold the souls of those who are dead, cry out.

11. And complain even to the gate of heaven.

---

[33] *Bring judgment to us from.*

12. Their groaning ascends; nor can they escape from the unrighteousness which is committed on earth. Thou knowest all things, before they exist.

13. Thou knowest these things, and what has been done by them; yet thou dost not speak to us.

14. What on account of these things ought we to do to them?

CHAP. X.

1. Then the Most High, the Great and Holy One spoke,

2. And sent Arsayalalyur to the son of Lamech,

3. Saying, Say to him in my name, Conceal thyself.

4. Then explain to him the consummation which is about to take place; for all the earth shall perish; the waters of a deluge shall come over the whole earth, and all things which are in it shall be destroyed.

5. And now teach him how he may escape, and how his seed may remain in all the earth.

6. Again the Lord said to Raphael, Bind Azazyel hand and foot; cast him into darkness; and opening the desert which is in Dudael, cast him in there.

7. Throw upon him hurled and pointed stones, covering him with darkness;

8. There shall he remain for ever; cover his face, that he may not see the light.

9. And in the great day of judgment let him be cast into the fire.

10. Restore the earth, which the angels have corrupted; and announce life to it, that I may revive it.

11. All the sons of men shall not perish in consequence of every secret, by *which* the Watchers have destroyed, and which they have taught, their offspring.

12.   All the earth has been corrupted by the effects of the teaching[34] of Azazyel. To him therefore ascribe the whole crime.

13.   To Gabriel also the Lord said, Go to the biters, to the reprobates, to the children of fornication; and destroy the children of fornication, the offspring of the Watchers, from among men; bring them forth, and excite[35] them one against another. Let them perish by *mutual* slaughter; for length of days shall not be theirs.

14.   They shall all entreat thee, but their fathers shall not obtain *their wishes* respecting them; for they shall hope for eternal life, and that they may live, each of them, five hundred years.

15.   To Michael likewise the Lord said, Go and announce *his crime* to Samyaza, and to the others who are with him, who have been associated with women, that they might be polluted with all their impurity. And when all their sons shall be slain, when they shall see the perdition of their beloved, bind them for seventy generations underneath the earth, even to the day of judgment, and of consummation, until the judgment, *the effect of* which will last for ever, be completed.[36]

16.   Then shall they be taken away into the lowest depths of the fire in torments; and in confinement shall they be shut up for ever.

17.   Immediately after this shall he, together with them, burn and perish; they shall be bound until the consummation of many generations.

18.   Destroy all the souls addicted to dalliance, and the offspring of the Watchers, for they have tyrannized over mankind.

19. Let every oppressor perish from the face of the earth;

20. Let every evil work be destroyed;

21.   The plant of righteousness and of rectitude appear, and its produce[37] become a blessing.

22. Righteousness and rectitude shall be for ever planted with delight.

---

[34] *by the teaching of the work of Azazyel.*
[35] *send.*
[36] Here end the first two extracts made by Syncellus.
[37] and the work of righteousness and rectitude.

23.   And then shall all the saints give thanks, and live until they have begotten a thousand children, while the whole period of their youth, and their sabbaths shall be completed in peace. In those days all the earth shall be cultivated in righteousness; it shall be wholly planted with trees, and filled with benediction; every tree of delight shall be planted in it.

24.   In it shall vines be planted; and the vine which shall be planted in it shall yield fruit to satiety; every seed, which shall be sown in it, shall produce for one measure a thousand; and one measure of olives shall produce ten presses of oil.

25.   Purify the earth from all oppression, from all injustice, from all crime, from all impiety, and from all the pollution which is committed upon it. Exterminate them from the earth.

26.   Then shall all the children of men be righteous, and all nations shall pay me divine honours, and bless me; and all shall adore me.

27.   The earth shall be cleansed from all corruption, from every crime, from all punishment, and from all suffering; neither will I again send a deluge upon it from generation to generation for ever.

28.   In those days I will open the treasures of blessing which are in heaven, that I may cause them to descend upon earth, and upon all the works and labour of man.

29.   Peace and equity shall associate with the sons of men all the days of the world, in every generation of it.

(No CHAP. XI.[38])

CHAP. XII. [SECT. III.[39]]

1. Before all these things Enoch was concealed; nor did any one of the sons of men know where he was concealed, where he had been, and what had happened.

2. He was wholly engaged with the holy ones, and with the Watchers in his days.

[38] The Paris MS. makes the last two verses of the preceding chapter, the xi. chapter.
[39] Paris MS.

3. I, Enoch, was blessing the great Lord and King of peace.

4. And behold the Watchers called me Enoch the scribe.

5. Then *the Lord* said to me: Enoch, scribe of righteousness, go tell the Watchers of heaven, who have deserted the lofty sky, and their holy everlasting station, *who* have been polluted with women.

6. And have done as the sons of men do, by taking to themselves wives, and who have been greatly corrupted on the earth;

7. That on the earth they shall never obtain peace and remission of sin. For they shall not rejoice in their offspring; they shall behold the slaughter of their beloved; shall lament for the destruction of their sons; and shall petition for ever; but shall not obtain mercy and peace.

CHAP. XIII.

1. Then Enoch, passing on, said to Azazyel: Thou shalt not obtain peace. A great sentence is gone forth against thee. He shall bind thee;

2. Neither shall relief, mercy, and supplication be thine, on account of the oppression which thou hast taught;

3. And on account of every act of blasphemy, tyranny, and sin, which thou hast discovered to the children of men.

4. Then departing from him I spoke to them all together;

5. And they all became terrified, and trembled;

6. Beseeching me to write for them a memorial of supplication, that they might obtain forgiveness; and that I might make the memorial of their prayer ascend up before the God of heaven; because they could not themselves thenceforwards address him, nor raise up their eyes to heaven on account of the disgraceful offence for which they were judged.

7. Then I wrote a memorial of their prayer and supplication, for their spirits, for everything which they had done, and for the subject of their entreaty, that they might obtain remission and rest.

8. Proceeding on, I continued over the waters of Danbadan, which is on the right to the west of Armon, reading the memorial of their prayer, until I fell asleep.

9. And behold a dream came to me, and visions appeared above me. I fell down and saw a vision of punishment, that I might relate it to the sons of heaven, and reprove them. When I awoke I went to them. All being collected together stood weeping in Oubelseyael, which is situated between Libanos and Seneser, with their faces veiled.

10. I related in their presence all the visions which I had seen, and my dream;

11. And began to utter these words of righteousness, reproving the Watchers of heaven.

CHAP. XIV.

1. This is the book of the words of righteousness, and of the reproof of the Watchers, who belong to the world, according to that which He, who is holy and great, commanded in the vision. I perceived in my dream, that I was now speaking with a tongue of flesh, and with my breath, which the Mighty One has put into the mouth of men, that they might converse with it.

2. And understand with the heart. As he has created and given to men *the power of* comprehending the word of understanding, so has he created and given to me *the power of* reproving the Watchers, the offspring of heaven. I have written your petition; and in my vision it has been shown me, that what you request will not be granted you as long as the world endures.[40]

3. Judgment has been passed upon you: *your request* will not be granted you.

4. From this time forward, never shall you ascend into heaven; He has said, that on the earth He will bind you, as long as the world endures.

---

[40] *in all the days of the world.*

5. But before these things you shall behold the destruction of your beloved sons; you shall not possess them, but they shall fall before you by the sword.

6. Neither shall you entreat for them, nor for yourselves;

7. But you shall weep and supplicate in silence. The words of the book which I wrote.

8. A vision thus appeared to me.

9. Behold, in *that* vision clouds and a mist invited me;[41] agitated stars[42] and flashes of lightning impelled and pressed me forwards, while winds in the vision assisted my flight, accelerating my progress.[43]

10. They elevated me aloft to heaven. I proceeded, until I arrived at a wall built with stones of crystal.[44] A vibrating flame[45] surrounded it, which began to strike me with terror.

11. Into this vibrating flame I entered;

12. And drew nigh to a spacious habitation built also with stones of crystal. Its walls too, as well as pavement, were *formed* with stones of crystal, and crystal likewise was the ground. Its roof had the appearance of agitated[46] stars and flashes of lightning; and among them were cherubim of fire in a stormy sky.[47] A flame burned around its walls; and its portal blazed with fire. When I entered into this dwelling, it was hot as fire and cold as ice. No *trace* of delight or of life was there. Terror overwhelmed me, and a fearful shaking seized me.

13. Violently agitated and trembling, I fell upon my face. In the vision I looked,

14. And behold there was another habitation more spacious than *the former*, every entrance to which was open before me, erected in *the midst of* a vibrating flame.

[41] *clouds invited me, and a mist invited me.*
[42] *the running of the stars.*
[43] *hastening me.*
[44] *hail, crystal.*
[45] *a tongue of fire.*
[46] *the course of the.*
[47] *and their heaven (i.e. whose heaven) was water.*

15.   So greatly did it excel in all points, in glory, in magnificence, and in magnitude, that it is impossible to describe to you either the splendour or the extent of it.

16.   Its floor was on fire; above were lightnings and agitated stars, while its roof exhibited a blazing fire.

17. Attentively I surveyed it, and saw that it contained an exalted throne;

18.   The appearance of which was like that of frost; while its circumference resembled the orb of the brilliant sun; and *there was* the voice of the cherubim.

19. From underneath this mighty throne rivers of flaming fire issued.

20. To look upon it was impossible.

21. One great in glory sat upon it:

22. Whose robe was brighter than the sun, and whiter than snow.

23.   No angel was capable of penetrating to view the face of Him, the Glorious and the Effulgent; nor could any mortal behold Him. A fire was flaming[48] around Him.

24.   A fire also of great extent continued to rise up before Him; so that not one of those who surrounded Him was capable of approaching Him, among the myriads of 'myriads who were before Him. To Him holy consultation was needless.[49] Yet did not the sanctified, who were near Him, depart far from Him either by night or by day; nor were they removed from Him. I also was so far advanced, with a veil on my face, and trembling. Then the Lord with his *own* mouth called me, saying, Approach hither, Enoch, at my holy word.

25.   And He raised me up, making me draw near even to the entrance. My eye was directed to the ground.

[48] *A fire of flaming fire.*
[49] *And he required not holy counsel.*

CHAP. XV.

1. Then addressing me, He spoke and said,[50] Hear, neither be afraid, O righteous Enoch, thou scribe of righteousness:[51] approach hither, and hear my voice. Go, say to the Watchers of heaven, who have sent thee to pray for them, You ought to pray for men, and not men for you.

2. Wherefore have you forsaken the lofty and holy heaven, which endures for ever, and have lain with women; have defiled yourselves with the daughters of men; have taken to yourselves wives; have acted like the sons of the earth, and have begotten an impious offspring?[52]

3. You being spiritual, holy, and possessing a life[53] which is eternal, have polluted yourselves with women; have begotten in carnal blood; have lusted in the blood of men; and have done as those who are flesh and blood do.

4. These however die and perish.

5. Therefore have I given to them wives, that they might cohabit with them; that sons might be born of them; and that this might be transacted upon earth.

6. But you from the beginning were made spiritual, possessing a life which is eternal, and not subject to death for ever.[54]

7. Therefore I made not wives for you, because, being spiritual, your dwelling is in heaven.

8.[55] Now the giants, who lave been born of spirit and of flesh, shall be called upon earth evil spirits, and on earth shall be their habitation. Evil spirits shall proceed from their flesh, because they were created from above; from the holy Watchers was their beginning and primary foundation. Evil spirits shall they be upon earth, and the spirits of the wicked shall they be called. The habitation of the spirits of heaven shall be in heaven; but upon earth shall be the habitation of terrestrial spirits, who are born on earth.

[50] *he said with his voice.*
[51] *O Enoch, O righteous man, and scribe of righteousness.*
[52] *giants.*
[53] *living a life.*
[54] *in all the generations of the world.*
[55] The third extract made by Syncellus begins here, and ends with the first verse of the next chapter.

9. The spirits of the giants shall be like clouds, which shall oppress, corrupt, fall, contend, and bruise upon earth.

10.   They shall cause lamentation. No food shall they eat; and they shall be thirsty; they shall be concealed, and shall not[56] rise up against the sons of men, and against women; for they come forth during the days of slaughter and destruction.

XVI

CHAP. XVI.

1. And as to the death of the giants, wheresoever their spirits depart from their bodies, let their flesh, that which is perishable, be without judgment. Thus shall they perish, until the day of the great consummation of the great world. A destruction shall take place of[57] the Watchers and the impious.

2. And now to the Watchers, who have sent thee to pray for them, who in the beginning were in heaven,

3. Say, In heaven have you been; secret things, however, have not been manifested to you; yet have you known a reprobated mystery.

4. And this you have related to women in the hardness of your heart, and by that mystery have women and mankind multiplied evils upon the earth.

5. Say to them, Never therefore shall you obtain peace.

CHAP. XVII. [SECT. IV.[58]]

1. They raised me up into a certain place,[59] where there was the appearance of a burning fire; and when they pleased they assumed the likeness of men.

---

[56] *and those spirits shall not.* M. De Sacy here remarks, that the sense seems to require an affirmative, instead of a negative, clause.
[57] *It shall be consummated respecting.*
[58] Paris MS., in which however the title of chap. xvii. is omitted, although the section is noticed.
[59] *one place.*

2. They carried me to a lofty spot, to a mountain, the top of which reached to heaven.

3. And I beheld the receptacles of light and of thunder at the extremities of the place, where it was deepest. There was a bow of fire, and arrows in their quiver, a sword of fire, and every species of lightning.

4. Then they elevated me to a babbling stream,[60] and to a fire in the west, which received all the setting of the sun. I came to a river of fire, which flowed like water, and emptied itself into the great sea westwards.

5. I saw every large river, until I arrived at the great darkness. I went to where all of flesh migrate; and I beheld the mountains of the gloom which constitutes winter, and the place from which issues the water in every abyss.

6. I saw also the mouths of all the rivers in the world, and the mouths of the deep.

CHAP. XVIII.

1. I then surveyed the receptacles of all the winds, perceiving that they contributed to adorn[61] the whole creation, and to preserve the foundation of the earth.

2. I surveyed the stone which supports the corners of the earth.

3. I also beheld the four winds, which bear up the earth, and the firmament of heaven.

4. And I beheld the winds occupying the exalted sky.[62]

5. Arising in the midst of heaven and of earth, and constituting the pillars of heaven.

6. I saw the winds which turn the sky, which cause the orb of the sun and of all the stars to set; and over the earth I saw the winds which support the clouds.

---

[60] *to water of life, which spoke.*
[61] *that in them were the ornaments of.*
[62] *the height of heaven.*

7. I saw the path of the angels.

8. I perceived at the extremity of the earth the firmament of heaven above it. Then I passed on towards the south;

9. Where burnt, both by day and night, six mountains formed of glorious stones; three towards the east, and three towards the south.

10. Those which were towards the east were of a variegated stone; one of which was of margarite, and another of antimony. Those towards the south were of a red stone. The middle one reached to heaven like the throne of God; *a throne composed* of alabaster, the top of which was of sapphire. I saw, too, a blazing fire hanging over[63] all the mountains.

11. And there I saw a place on the other side of an extended territory, where waters were collected.

12. I likewise beheld terrestrial fountains, deep in the fiery columns of heaven.

13. And in the columns of heaven I beheld fires, which descended without number, but neither on high, nor into the deep. Over these fountains also I perceived a place which had neither the firmament of heaven above it, nor the solid ground underneath it; neither was there water above it, nor anything on wing; but the spot was desolate.

14. And there I beheld seven stars, like great blazing mountains, and like spirits entreating me.

15. Then the angel said, This place, until the consummation of heaven and earth, will be the prison of the stars, and the host of heaven.

16. The stars which roll over fire are those which transgressed the commandment of God before their time arrived; for they came not in their proper season. Therefore was He offended with them, and bound them, until the period of the consummation of their crimes in the secret year.

[63] *which was over.*

CHAP. XIX.

1. Then Uriel said, Here the angels, who cohabited with women, appointed their leaders;

2. And being numerous in appearance made men profane, and caused them to err; so that they sacrificed to devils as to gods. For in the great day *there shall be* a judgment, with which they shall be *judged*, until they are consumed; and their wives also shall be judged, who led astray the angels of heaven that they might salute them.

3. And I, Enoch, I alone saw the likeness of the end of all things. Nor did any human being see it, as I saw it.

CHAP. XX.

1. These are the names of the angels who watch.

2. Uriel, one of the holy angels, who *presides* over[64] clamour and terror.

3. Raphael, one of the holy angels, who *presides* over the spirits of men.

4. Raguel, one of the holy angels, who inflicts punishment on the world and the luminaries.

5. Michael, one of the holy angels, who, *presiding* over human virtue, commands the nations.

6. Sarakiel, one of the holy angels, who *presides* over the spirits of the children of men that transgress.

7. Gabriel, one of the holy angels, who *presides* over Ikisat,[65] over paradise, and over the cherubim.

---

[64] *for* he it is *who* is over.
[65] *Ikisat.* This appears to be a proper name.

CHAPTERS XXI-XL

CHAP. XXI.

1. Then I made a circuit to a place in which nothing was completed.

2. And there I beheld neither the tremendous workmanship of an exalted heaven, nor of an established earth, but a desolate spot, prepared, and terrific.

3. There, too, I beheld seven stars of heaven bound in it together, like great mountains, and like a blazing fire. I exclaimed, For what species of crime have they been bound, and why have they been removed to this place? Then Uriel, one of the holy angels who was with me, and who conducted me, answered: Enoch, wherefore dost thou ask; wherefore reason with thyself, and anxiously inquire? These are those of the stars which have transgressed the commandment of the most high God; and are here bound, until the infinite number of the days of their crimes be completed.

4. From thence I afterwards passed on to another terrific place;

5. Where I beheld the operation of a great fire blazing and glittering, in the midst of which there was a division. Columns of fire struggled together to the end of the abyss, and deep was their descent. But neither its measurement nor magnitude was I able to discover; neither could I perceive its origin. Then I exclaimed, How terrible is this place, and how difficult to explore!

6. Uriel, one of the holy angels who was with me, answered and said: Enoch, why art thou alarmed and amazed at this terrific place, at the sight of this *place of* suffering? This, he said, is the prison of the angels; and here they are kept for ever.

CHAP. XXII. [SECT. V.⁶⁶]

1. From thence I proceeded to another spot, where I saw on the west a great and lofty mountain, a strong rock, and four delightful places.

2. Internally it was deep, capacious, and very smooth; as smooth as if it had been rolled over: it was both deep and dark to behold.

3. Then Raphael, one of the holy angels who were with me, answered and said, These are the delightful places where the spirits, the souls of the dead, will be collected; for them were they formed; and here will be collected all the souls of the sons of men.

4. These places, in which they dwell, shall they occupy until the day of judgment, and until their appointed period.

5. Their appointed period will be long, even until the great judgment. And I saw the spirits of the sons of men who were dead; and their voices reached to heaven, while they were accusing.⁶⁷

6. Then I inquired of Raphael, an angel who was with me, and said, Whose spirit is that, the voice of which reaches *to heaven*, and accuses?

7. He answered, saying, This is the spirit of Abel, who was slain by Cain his brother; and who will accuse that brother,⁶⁸ until his seed be destroyed from the face of the earth;

8. Until his seed perish from the seed of the human race.

9. At that time therefore I inquired respecting him, and respecting the general judgment, saying, Why is one separated from another? He answered, Three *separations* have been made between the spirits of the dead, and thus have the spirits of the righteous been separated.

10. Namely, *by* a chasm, *by* water, and *by* light above it.

11. And in the same way likewise are sinners separated when they die, and are buried in the earth; judgment not overtaking them in their lifetime.

---

⁶⁶ Paris MS.
⁶⁷ *blaming or reproving.*
⁶⁸ *and he will accuse him.*

12. Here their souls are separated. Moreover, abundant is their suffering until the time of the great judgment, the castigation, and the torment of those who eternally execrate, whose souls are punished and bound there for ever.

13. And thus has it been front the beginning of the world. Thus has there existed a separation between the souls of those who utter complaints, and of those who watch for their destruction, to slaughter them in the day of sinners.

14. A receptacle of this sort has been formed[69] for the souls of unrighteous men, and of sinners; of those who have completed crime, and associated with the impious, whom they resemble. Their souls shall not be annihilated in the day of judgment, neither shall they arise from this place. Then I blessed God,

15. And said, Blessed be my Lord, the Lord of glory and of righteousness, who reigns over all for ever and for ever.

CHAP. XXIII.

1. From thence I went to another place, towards the west, unto the extremities of the earth.

2. Where I beheld a fire blazing and running along without cessation, which intermitted its course neither by day nor by night; but continued always the same.

3. I inquired, saying, What is this, which never ceases?

4. Then Raguel, one of the holy angels who were with me, answered,

5. And said, This blazing fire, which thou beholdest running towards the west, is *that of* all the luminaries of heaven.

[69] *Thus has it been made.*

CHAP. XXIV.

1. I went from thence to another place, and saw a mountain of fire flashing both by day and night. I proceeded towards it; and perceived seven splendid mountains, which were all different from each other.

2. Their stones were brilliant and beautiful; all were brilliant and splendid to behold; and beautiful was their surface.
Three *mountains* were towards the east, and strengthened by being placed one upon another; and three were towards the south, strengthened in a similar manner. There were likewise deep valleys, which did not approach each other. And the seventh mountain was in the midst of them. In length they all resembled the seat of a throne, and odoriferous trees surrounded them.

3. Among these there was a tree of an unceasing smell; nor of those which were in Eden was there one of all the fragrant trees which smelt like this. Its leaf, its flower, and its bark never withered, and its fruit was beautiful.

4. Its fruit resembled the cluster of the palm. I exclaimed, Behold! this tree is goodly in aspect, pleasing in its leaf, and the sight of its fruit is delightful to the eye. Then Michael, one of the holy and glorious angels who were with me, and one who presided over them, answered,

5. And said: Enoch, why dost thou inquire respecting the odour of this tree?

6. *Why* art thou inquisitive to know it?

7. Then I, Enoch, replied to him, and said, Concerning everything I am desirous of instruction, but particularly concerning this tree.

8. He answered me, saying, That mountain which thou beholdest, the extent of whose head resembles the seat of the Lord, will be the seat on which shall sit the holy and great Lord of glory, the everlasting King, when he shall come and descend to visit the earth with goodness.

9. And that tree of an agreeable smell, not one of carnal *odour*,[70] there shall be no power to touch, until the period of the great judgment. When

[70] *of flesh.*

all shall be punished and consumed for ever, this shall be bestowed on the righteous and humble. The fruit of this *tree* shall be given to the elect. For towards the north life shall be planted in the holy place, towards the habitation of the everlasting King.

10.   Then shall they greatly rejoice and exult in the Holy One. The sweet odour shall enter into their bones; and they shall live a long life on the earth, as thy forefathers have lived; neither in their days shall sorrow, distress, trouble, and punishment afflict them.

11.   And I blessed the Lord of glory, the everlasting King, because He has prepared *this tree* for the saints, formed it, and declared that He would give it to them.

CHAP. XXV.

1. From thence I proceeded to the middle of the earth, and beheld a happy and fertile spot, which contained branches continually sprouting from the trees which were planted in it. There I saw a holy mountain, and underneath it water on the eastern side, which flowed towards the south. I saw also on the east another mountain as high as that; and between them there were deep, but not wide valleys.

2. Water ran towards the mountain to the west of this; and underneath there was likewise another mountain.

3. There was a valley, but not a wide one, below it; and in the midst of them were other deep and dry valleys towards the extremity of the three. All these valleys, which were deep, but not wide, consisted of a strong rock, with a tree which was planted in them. And I wondered at the rock and at the valleys, being extremely surprised.

CHAP. XXVI.

1. Then I said, What means this blessed land, all these lofty trees, and the accursed valley between them?

2. Then Uriel, one of the holy angels who were with me, replied, This valley is the accursed of the accursed for ever. Here shall be collected all

who utter with their mouths unbecoming language against God, and speak harsh things of His glory. Here shall they be collected. Here shall be their territory.

3. In the latter days an example of judgment shall be made of them in righteousness before the saints: while those who have received mercy shall for ever, all their days, bless God, the everlasting King.

4. And at the period of judgment shall they bless Him for his mercy, as He has distributed it to them. Then I blessed God, addressing myself to Him, and making mention, as was meet, of His greatness.

CHAP. XXVII.

1. From thence I proceeded towards the east, to the middle of the mountain in the desert, the level surface only of which I perceived.

2. It was full of trees of the seed alluded to; and water leaped down upon it.

3. There appeared a cataract composed as of many cataracts both towards the west and towards the east. Upon one side were trees; upon the other water and dew.

CHAP. XXVIII.

1. Then I went to another place from the desert, towards the east of that mountain *which* I had approached.

2. There I beheld choice trees, particularly *those which produce* the sweet-smelling drugs, frankincense and myrrh;[71] and trees unlike to each other.

3. And over it, above them, was the elevation of the eastern mountain at no great distance.

---

[71] *trees of judgment, particularly furniture of the sweet smell of frankincense and myrrh.*

CHAP. XXIX.

1. I likewise saw another place with valleys of water which never wasted,

2. *Where* I perceived a goodly tree, which in smell resembled Zasakinon.

3. And towards the sides of these valleys I perceived cinnamon of a sweet odour. Over them I advanced towards the east.

CHAP. XXX.

1. Then I beheld another mountain containing trees, from which water flowed like Neketro. Its name was Sarira, and Kalboneba. And upon this mountain I beheld another mountain, upon which were trees of Alva.

2. These trees were full, like almond trees, anal strong; and when they produced fruit, it was superior to all perfume.

CHAP. XXXI.

1. After these things, surveying the entrances of the north, above the mountains, I perceived seven mountains replete with pure nard, odoriferous trees, cinnamon and papyrus.

2. From thence I passed on above the summits of those mountains to some distance eastwards, and went over the Erythræan sea. And when I was advanced far beyond it, I passed along above the angel Zateel, and arrived at the garden of righteousness. In this garden I beheld, among other trees, some which were numerous and large, and which flourished there.

3. Their fragrance was agreeable and powerful,[72] and their appearance both varied and elegant. The tree of knowledge also was there, of which if any one eats, he becomes endowed with great wisdom.

4. It was like a species of the tamarind tree, bearing fruit which resembled grapes extremely fine; and its fragrance extended to a

[72] *good and great.*

considerable distance. I exclaimed, How beautiful is this tree, and how delightful is its appearance!

5. Then holy Raphael, an angel who was with me, answered and said, This is the tree of knowledge, of which thy ancient father and thy aged mother ate, who were before thee; and who, obtaining knowledge, their eyes being opened, and knowing themselves to be naked, were expelled from the garden.

CHAP. XXXII.

1. From thence I went on towards the extremities of the earth; where I saw large beasts different from each other, and birds various in their countenances and forms, as well as with notes of different sounds.

2. To the east of these beasts I perceived the extremities of the earth, where heaven ceased. The gates of heaven stood open, and I beheld the celestial stars come forth. I numbered them as they proceeded out of the gate, and wrote them all down, as they came out one by one according to their number. *I wrote down* their names altogether, their times and their seasons, as the angel Uriel, who was with me, pointed them out to me.

3. He showed them all to me, and wrote down *an account of* them.

4. He also wrote down for me their names, their regulations, and their operations.

CHAP. XXXIII.

1. From thence I advanced on towards the north, to the extremities of the earth.

2. And there I saw a great and glorious wonder at the extremities of the whole earth.

3. I saw there heavenly gates opening into heaven; three of them distinctly separated. The northern winds proceeded from them, blowing cold, hail, frost, snow, dew, and rain.

4. From one of the gates they blew mildly; but when they blew from the two *other gates*, it was with violence and force. They blew over the earth strongly.

CHAP. XXXIV.

1. From thence I went to the extremities of the world westwards;

2. Where I perceived three gates open, as I had seen in the north; the gates and passages through them being of equal magnitude.

CHAP. XXXV.

1. Then I proceeded to the extremities of the earth southwards; where I saw three gates open to the south, from which issued dew, rain, and wind.

2. From thence I went to the extremities of heaven eastwards; where I saw three heavenly gates open to the east, which had smaller gates within them. Through each of these small gates the stars of heaven passed on, and proceeded towards the west by a path which was seen by them, and that at every period *of their appearance.*

3. When I beheld *them*, I blessed; every time *in which they appeared*, I blessed the Lord of glory, who had made those great and splendid signs, that they might display the magnificence of his works to angels and to the souls of men; and that these might glorify all his works and operations; might see the effect of his power; might glorify the great labour of his hands; and bless him for ever.

CHAP. XXXVII.[73] [SECT. VI.[74]]

1. The vision which he saw, the second vision of wisdom, which Enoch saw, the son of Jared, the son of Malaleel, the son of Canan, the son of Enos, the son of Seth, the son of Adam. This is the commencement of the

[73] Chap. xxxvi. does not occur in the MS.
[74] Paris MS. and Bodleian MS.

word of wisdom, which I received to declare and tell to those who dwell upon earth. Hear from the beginning, and understand to the end, the holy things which I utter in the presence of the Lord of spirits. Those who were before *us* thought it good to speak;

2. And let not us, who come after, obstruct the beginning of wisdom. Until the present period never has there been given before the Lord of spirits that which I have received, wisdom according to the capacity of my intellect,[75] and according to the pleasure of the Lord of spirits; that which I have received from him,[76] a portion of life eternal.

3. And I obtained three parables, which I declared to the inhabitants of the world.

CHAP. XXXVIII.

1. Parable the first. When the congregation of the righteous shall be manifested; and sinners be judged for their crimes, and be troubled in the sight of the world;

2. When righteousness shall be manifested in the presence of the righteous themselves, who will be elected for their *good* works *duly* weighed by the Lord of spirits; and when the light of the righteous and the elect, who dwell on earth, shall be manifested; where will the habitation of sinners be? and where the place of rest for those who have rejected the Lord of spirits? It would have been better for them, had they never been born.

3. When, too, the secrets of the righteous shall be revealed, then shall sinners be judged; and impious men shall be afflicted in the presence of the righteous and the elect.

4. From that period those who possess the earth shall cease to be[77] powerful and exalted. Neither shall they be capable of beholding the countenances of the holy; for the light of the countenances of the holy, the righteous, and the elect, has been seen by the Lord of spirits.

---

[75] *according as I have thought.*
[76] *which has been given to me by him.*
[77] *shall not be.*

5. Yet shall not the mighty kings of that period be destroyed; but be delivered into the hands of the righteous and the holy.

6. Nor thenceforwards shall any obtain commiseration from the Lord of spirits, because their lives *in this world* will have been completed.

CHAP. XXXIX.

1. In those days shall the elect and holy race descend from the upper heavens, and their seed shall then be with the sons of men. Enoch received books of indignation and wrath, and books of hurry and agitation.

2. Never shall they obtain mercy, saith the Lord of spirits.

3. A cloud then snatched me up, and the wind raised me above the surface of the earth, placing me at the extremity of the heavens.

4. There I saw another vision; I *saw* the habitations and couches of the saints. There my eyes beheld their habitations with the angels, and their couches with the holy ones. They were entreating, supplicating, and praying for the sons of men; while righteousness like water flowed before them, and mercy like dew *was scattered* over the earth. And thus *shall it be* with them for ever and for ever.

5. At that time my eyes beheld the dwelling[78] of the elect, of truth, faith, and righteousness.

6. Countless shall be the number of the holy and the elect, in the presence of God[79] for ever and for ever.

7. Their residence I beheld under the wings of the Lord of spirits. All the holy and the elect sung before him, in appearance like a blaze of fire; their mouths being full of blessings, and their lips glorifying the name of the Lord of spirits. And righteousness incessantly *dwelt* before him,

8. There was I desirous of remaining, and my soul longed for that habitation. There was my antecedent inheritance; for thus had I prevailed[80] before the Lord of spirits.

[78] *place.*
[79] *in his presence.*

9. At that time I glorified and extolled the name of the Lord of spirits with blessing and with praise; for he has established it with blessing and with praise, according to his own good pleasure.[81]

10. That place long did my eyes contemplate. I blessed and said, Blessed be he, blessed from the beginning for ever. In the beginning, before the world was created, and without end is his knowledge.[82]

11. What is this world? Of every existing generation those shall bless thee who do not sleep *in the dust*, but stand before thy glory, blessing, glorifying, exalting thee, and saying, The holy, holy, Lord of spirits, fills the whole world of spirits.

12. There my eyes beheld all who, without sleeping, stand before him and bless him, saying, Blessed be thou, and blessed be the name of God for ever and for ever. Then my countenance became changed, until I was incapable of seeing.

CHAP. XL.

1. After this I beheld thousands of thousands, and myriads of myriads, and an infinite number of people, standing before the Lord of spirits.

2. On the four wings likewise of the Lord of spirits, on the four sides, I perceived others, besides those who were standing *before him*. Their names, too, I know; because the angel, who proceeded with me, declared them to me, discovering to me every secret thing.

3. Then I heard the voices of those upon the four sides magnifying the Lord of glory.

4. The first voice blessed the Lord of spirits for ever and for ever.

5. The second voice I heard blessing the elect One, and the elect who suffer[83] on account of the Lords of spirits.

---

[80] *There was my portion before; for thus had it been prevailed respecting me.*
[81] *according to the will of the Lord of spirits.*
[82] *without end he knows.*
[83] *are crucified or tormented.*

6. The third voice I heard petitioning and praying for those who dwell upon earth, and supplicate the name of the Lord of spirits.

7. The fourth voice I heard expelling the impious angels,[84] and prohibiting them from entering into presence of the Lord of spirits, to prefer accusations against the inhabitants of the earth.

8. After this I besought the angel of peace, who proceeded with me, to explain all that was concealed. I said to him, Who are those *whom* I have seen on the four sides, and whose words I have heard and written down? He replied, The first is the merciful, the patient, the holy Michael.

9. The second is he who *presides* over every suffering and every affliction[85] of the sons of men, the holy Raphael. The third, who *presides* over all that is powerful, is Gabriel. And the fourth, who *presides* over repentance, and the hope of those who will inherit eternal life, is Phanuel. These are the four angels of the most high God, and their four voices, which at that time I heard.

---

[84] *the Satans.*
[85] *wound.*

Chapters XLI-LX

CHAP. XLI.

1. After this I beheld the secrets of the heavens and of paradise,[86] according to its divisions; and of human action,[87] as they weigh it there in balances. I saw the habitations of the elect, and the habitations of the holy. And there my eyes beheld all the sinners, who denied the Lord of glory, and whom they were expelling from thence, and dragging away, as they stood *there*; no punishment proceeding against them from the Lord of spirits.

2. There, too, my eyes beheld the secrets of the lightning and the thunder; and the secrets of the winds, how they are distributed as they blow over the earth: the secrets of the winds, of the dew, and of the clouds. There I perceived the place from which they issued forth, and became saturated with the dust of the earth.

3. There I saw the wooden[88] receptacles out of which the winds became separated, the receptacle of hail, the receptacle of snow, the receptacle of the clouds, and the cloud itself, *which* continued over the earth before *the creation* of the world.

4. I beheld also the receptacles of the moon, whence the moons[89] came, whither they proceeded, their glorious return, and how one became more splendid than another. I *marked* their rich progress, their unchangeable progress, their disunited and undiminished progress; their observance of a mutual fidelity by a stable oath[90]; their proceeding forth before the sun, and their adherence to the path *allotted* them,[91] in obedience to the command of the Lord of spirits. Potent is his name for ever and for ever.

5. After this *I perceived, that* the path both concealed and manifest of the moon, as well as the progress of its path, was there completed by day and by night; while each, one with another, looked towards the Lord of

---

[86] *the kingdom or paradise.*
[87] *the work or labour of man.*
[88] *of woods.*
[89] *they.*
[90] *by an oath to which they adhered.*
[91] *to their path.*

spirits, magnifying and praising without cessation, since praise to them is rest; for in the splendid sun there is a frequent conversion to blessing and to malediction.

6. The course of the moon's path to the righteous is light, but to sinners it is darkness; in the name of the Lord of spirits, who created *a division* between light and darkness, and, separating the spirits of men, strengthened the spirits of the righteous in the name of his own righteousness.

7. Nor does the angel prevent *this*, neither is he endowed with the power of preventing it; for the Judge beholds them all, and judges them all in his own presence.

CHAP. XLII.

1. Wisdom found not a place *on earth* where she could inhabit; her dwelling therefore is in heaven.

2. Wisdom went forth to dwell among the sons of men, but she obtained not an habitation. Wisdom returned to her place, and seated herself in the midst of the angels. But iniquity went forth after her return, who unwillingly found *an habitation*, and resided among them, as rain in the desert, and as a dew in a thirsty land.

CHAP. XLIII.

1. I beheld another splendour, and the stars of heaven. I observed that he called them all by their respective names, and that they heard. In a righteous balance I saw that he weighed out with their light the amplitude of their places, and the day of their appearance,[92] and their conversion. Splendour produced splendour; and their conversion *was* into the number of the angels, and of the faithful.

2. Then I inquired of the angel, who proceeded with me, and explained to me secret things, What *their names* were. He answered, A similitude of those has the Lord of spirits shown thee. They are names of the righteous

---

[92] *of their existing.*

who dwell upon earth, and who believe in the name of the Lord of spirits for ever and for ever.

CHAP. XLIV.

Another thing also I saw respecting splendour; that it rises out of the stars, and becomes splendour; being incapable of forsaking them.

CHAP. XLV. [SECT. VII.[93]]

1. Parable the second, respecting these who deny[94] the name of the habitation of the holy ones, and of the Lord of spirits.

2. Heaven they shall not ascend, nor shall they come on the earth. This shall be the portion of sinners, who deny the name of the Lord of spirits, and who are thus reserved for the day of punishment and of affliction.

3. In that day shall the Elect One sit upon a throne of glory; and shall choose their conditions and countless habitations (while their spirits within them shall be strengthened, when they behold my Elect One), *shall choose them* for those who have fled for protection to my holy and glorious name.

4. In that day I will cause my Elect One to dwell in the midst of them; will change *the face of* heaven; will bless it, and illuminate it for ever.

5. I will also change *the face of* the earth; will bless it; and cause those whom I have elected to dwell upon it. But those who have committed sin and iniquity shall not inhabit it,[95] for I have marked their proceedings.[96] My righteous ones will I satisfy with peace, placing them before me; but the condemnation of sinners shall draw near, that I may destroy them from the face of the earth.

---

[93] In the Paris MS. it is section viii. In the Bodleian MS. section vii.
[94] In the Bodleian MS. there seems here an evident omission. This omission is supplied in the Paris MS. I have followed the latter.
[95] *tread upon it.*
[96] *for I have seen them.*

CHAP. XLVI.

1. There I beheld the Ancient of days,[97] whose head was like white wool, and with him another, whose countenance resembled that of man. His countenance was full of grace, like *that of* one of the holy angels. Then I inquired of one of the angels,[98] who went with me, and who showed me every secret thing, concerning this Son of man; who he was; whence he was; and why he accompanied the Ancient of days.

2. He answered and said to me, This is the Son of man, to whom righteousness belongs; with whom righteousness has dwelt; and who will reveal all the treasures of that which is concealed: for the Lord of spirits has chosen him; and his portion has surpassed[99] all before the Lord of spirits in everlasting uprightness.

3. This Son of man, whom thou beholdest, shall raise up kings and the mighty from their couches, and the powerful from their thrones; shall loosen the bridles of the powerful, and break in pieces the teeth of sinners.

4. He shall hurl kings from their thrones and their dominions; because they will not exalt and praise him, nor humble themselves *before him*, by whom[100] their kingdoms were granted to them. The countenance likewise of the mighty shall He cast down, filling them with confusion. Darkness shall be their habitation, and worms shall be their bed; nor from *that* their bed shall they hope to be again raised, because they exalted not the name of the Lord of spirits.

5. They shall condemn the stars of heaven, shall lift up their hands against the Most High, shall tread upon and inhabit the earth, exhibiting all their works of iniquity, even their works of iniquity. Their strength shall be in their riches, and their faith in the gods whom they have formed with their own hands. They shall deny the name of the Lord of spirits, and shall expel him from the temples, in which they assemble;

6. And *with him* the faithful, who suffer in the name of the Lord of spirits.

[97] *The Chief* or *Head of days*, Dan. vii. 9.
[98] The words, *Then I inquired of one of the angels*, are omitted in the Bodleian MS. They occur in the Paris MS.
[99] *conquered.*
[100] *from whence.*

CHAP. XLVII.

1. In that day the prayer of the holy and the righteous, and the blood of the righteous, shall ascend from the earth into the presence of the Lord of spirits.

2. In that day shall the holy ones assemble, who dwell above the heavens, and with united voice petition, supplicate, praise, laud, and bless the name of the Lord of spirits, on account of the blood of the righteous which has been shed; that the prayer of the righteous may not be intermitted before the Lord of spirits; that for them he would execute judgment; and that his patience may not endure for ever.

3. At that time I beheld the Ancient of days, while he sat upon the throne of his glory, *while* the book of the living was opened in his presence, and *while* all the powers which were above the heavens stood around and before him.

4. Then were the hearts of the saints full of joy, because the consummation[101] of righteousness was arrived, the supplication of the saints heard, and the blood of the righteous appreciated by the Lord of spirits.

CHAP. XLVIII.

1. In that place I beheld a fountain of righteousness, which never failed, encircled by many springs of wisdom. Of these all the thirsty drank, and were filled with wisdom, having their habitation with the righteous, the elect, and the holy.

2. In that hour was this Son of man invoked before the Lord of spirits, and his name in the presence of the Ancient of days.

3. Before the sun and the signs were created, before the stars of heaven were formed, his name was invoked in the presence of the Lord of spirits. A support shall he be for the righteous and the holy to lean upon, without falling; and he shall be the light of nations.

[101] *the number.*

4. He shall be the hope of those whose hearts are troubled. All, who dwell on earth, shall fall down and worship before him; shall bless and glorify him, and sing praises to the name of the Lord of spirits.

5. Therefore the Elect and the Concealed One existed in his presence, before the world was created, and for ever.

6. In his presence *he existed*, and has revealed to the saints and to the righteous the wisdom of the Lord of spirits; for he has preserved the lot of the righteous, because they have hated and rejected this world of iniquity, and have detested all its works and ways, in the name of the Lord of spirits.

7. For in his name shall they be preserved; and his will shall be their life. In those days shall the kings of the earth and the mighty men, who have gained the world by their achievements,[102] become humble in countenance.

8. For in the day of their anxiety and trouble their souls shall not be saved; and they shall be in subjection to[103] those whom I have chosen.

9. I will cast them like hay into the fire, and like lead into the water. Thus shall they burn in the presence of the righteous, and sink in the presence of the holy; nor shall a tenth part of them be found.

10. But in the day of their trouble, the world shall obtain tranquillity.[104]

11. In his presence shall they fall, and not be raised up again; nor shall there be any one to take them out of his hands, and to lift them up: for they have denied the Lord of spirits, and his Messiah. The name of the Lord of spirits shall be blessed.

CHAP. XLVIII.[105]

1. Wisdom is poured forth like water, and glory fails not before him for ever and ever; for potent is he in all the secrets of righteousness.

[102] *by the work of their own hands.*
[103] *in the hand of.*
[104] *rest shall be on earth.*
[105] Chap. xlviii. occurs twice.

2. But iniquity passes away like a shadow, and possesses not a fixed station: for the Elect One stands before the Lord of spirits; and his glory is for ever and ever; and his power from generation to generation.

3. With him dwells the spirit of intellectual wisdom, the spirit of instruction and of power, and the spirit of those who sleep in righteousness; he shall judge secret things.

4. Nor shall any be able to utter a single word before him; for the Elect One is in the presence of the Lord of spirits, according to his own pleasure.

CHAP. XLIX.

1. In those days the saints and the chosen shall undergo a change. The light of day shall rest upon them; and the splendour and glory of the saints shall be changed.

2. In the day of trouble evil shall be heaped up upon sinners; but the righteous shall triumph in the name of the Lord of spirits.

3. Others shall be made to see, that they must repent, and forsake the works of their hands; and that glory awaits them not in the presence of the Lord of spirits; yet that by his name they may be saved. The Lord of spirits will have compassion on them: for great is his mercy; and righteousness is in his judgment, and in the presence of his glory; nor in his judgment shall iniquity stand. He who repents not before him shall perish.

4. Henceforward I will not have mercy on them, saith the Lord of spirits.

CHAP. L.

1. In those days shall the earth deliver up from her womb, and hell deliver up from hers, that which it has received; and destruction shall restore that which it owes.

2. He shall select the righteous and holy from among them; for the day of their salvation has approached.

3. And in those days shall the Elect One sit upon his throne, while every secret of intellectual wisdom shall proceed from his mouth; for the Lord of spirits has gifted and glorified him.

4. In those days the mountains shall skip like rams, and the hills shall leap like young sheep[106] satiated with milk; and all *the righteous* shall become angels in heaven.

5. Their countenance shall be bright with joy; for in those days shall the Elect One be exalted. The earth shall rejoice; the righteous shall inhabit it, and the elect possess it.[107]

CHAP. LI.

1. After that period, in the place where I had seen every secret sight, I was snatched up in a whirlwind, and carried off westwards.

2. There my eyes beheld the secrets of heaven, and all which existed on earth; a mountain of iron, a mountain of copper,[108] a mountain of silver, a mountain of gold, a mountain of fluid metal, and a mountain of lead.

3. And I inquired of the angel who went with me, saying, What are these things, which in secret I behold?

4. He said, All these things which thou beholdest shall be for the dominion of the Messiah, that he may command, and be powerful upon earth.

5. And that angel of peace answered me, saying, Wait but a short time, and thou shalt understand, and every secret thing shall be revealed to thee, which the Lord of spirits has decreed. Those mountains which thou hast seen, the mountain of iron, the mountain of copper, the mountain of silver, the mountain of gold, the mountain of fluid metal, and the mountain of lead, all these in the presence of the Elect One shall be like a honeycomb before the fire, and like water descending from above upon these mountains; and shall become debilitated before his feet.

6. In those days men[109] shall not be saved by gold and by silver.

[106] Psalm cxiv. 4.
[107] *go and walk upon it.*
[108] *nummus minutissimus. Obolus.*

7. Nor shall they have it in their power to secure themselves, and to fly.

8. There shall be neither iron for war, nor a coat of mail for the breast.

9. Copper shall be useless; useless also that which neither rusts nor consumes away; and lead shall not be coveted.

10. All these things shall be rejected, and perish from off the earth, when the Elect One shall appear in the presence of the Lord of spirits.

CHAP. LII.

1. There my eyes beheld a deep valley; and wide was its entrance.

2. All who dwell on land, on the sea, and in islands, shall bring to it gifts, presents, and offerings; yet that deep valley shall not be full. Their hands shall commit iniquity. Whatsoever they produce by labour, the sinners shall devour with crime. But they shall perish front the face of the Lord of spirits, and from the face of his earth. They shall stand up, and shall not fail for ever and ever.

3. I beheld the angels of punishment, who were dwelling *there*, and preparing every instrument of Satan.

4. Then I inquired of the angel of peace, who proceeded with me, for whom those instruments were preparing.

5. He said, These they are preparing for the kings and powerful ones of the earth, that thus[110] they may perish.

6. After which the righteous and chosen house of his congregation shall appear, thenceforward unchangeable, in the name of the Lord of spirits.

7. Nor shall those mountains exist in his presence, as the earth and the hills, as the fountains of water exist. And the righteous shall be relieved from the vexation of sinners.

[109] *they.*
[110] *by this.*

CHAP. LIII.

1. Then I looked and turned myself to another part of the earth, where I beheld a deep valley burning with fire.

2. To this valley they brought monarchs and the mighty.

3. And there my eyes beheld the instruments which they were making, fetters of iron without weight.[111]

4. Then I inquired of the angel of peace, who proceeded with me, saying, For whom are these fetters and instruments prepared?

5. He replied, These are prepared for the host of Azazeel, that they may be delivered over and adjudged to the lowest condemnation; and that their angels may be overwhelmed with hurled stones, as the Lord of spirits has commanded.

6. Michael and Gabriel, Raphael and Phanuel shall be strengthened in that day, and shall then cast them into a furnace of blazing fire, that the Lord of spirits may be avenged of them for their crimes; because they became ministers of Satan, and seduced those who dwell upon earth.

7. In those days shall punishment go forth from the Lord of spirits; and the receptacles of water which are above the heavens shall be opened, and the fountains likewise, which are under the heavens and under the earth.

8. All the waters, which are in the heavens and above them, shall be mixed together.

9. The water which is above heaven shall be the agent;[112]

10. And the water which is under the earth shall be the recipient[113]: and all shall be destroyed who dwell upon earth, and who dwell under the extremities of heaven.

11. By these means shall they understand the iniquity which they have committed on earth: and by these means shall they perish.

---

[111] *in which there was not weight.*
[112] *male.*
[113] *female.*

CHAP. LIV.

1. Afterwards the Ancient of days repented, and said, In vain have I destroyed all the inhabitants of the earth.

2. And he sware by his great name, *saying*, Henceforwards I will not act thus towards all those who dwell upon earth.

3. But I will place a sign in the heavens;[114] and it shall be a faithful witness[115] between me and them for ever, as long as the days of heaven and earth last upon the earth.

4. Afterwards, according to this my decree, when I shall be disposed to seize them beforehand, by the instrumentality of angels, in the day of affliction and trouble, my wrath and my punishment shall remain upon them, my punishment and my wrath, saith God the Lord of spirits.

5. O ye kings, O ye mighty, who inhabit the world, you shall behold my Elect One, sitting upon the throne of my glory. And he shall judge Azazeel, all his associates, and all his hosts, in the name of the Lord of spirits.

6. There likewise I beheld hosts of angels who were moving in punishment, confined in a net-work of iron and brass. Then I inquired of the angel of peace, who proceeded with me, To whom those under confinement were going.

7. He said, To each of their elect and their beloved, that they may be cast into the fountains and deep recesses of the valley.

8. And that valley shall be filled with their elect and beloved; the days of whose life shall be consumed, but the days of their error shall be innumerable.

9. Then shall princes combine together, and conspire. The chiefs of the east, among the Parthians and Medes, shall remove kings, in whom a spirit of perturbation shall enter. They shall hurl them from their

---

[114] Gen. ix. 12. "I do set my bow in the cloud, and it shall be for a token of a covenant between me and the earth."
[115] *faith*, or *fidelity*.

thrones, springing as lions from their dens, and like famished wolves into the midst of the flock.

10.   They shall go up, and tread upon the land of their elect. The land of their elect shall be before them. The threshing-floor, the path, and the city of my righteous *people* shall impede *the progress of* their horses. They shall rise up to destroy each other; their right hand shall be strengthened; nor shall a man acknowledge his friend or his brother;

11.   Nor the son his father and his mother; until the number of the dead bodies shall be *completed*, by their death and punishment. Neither shall this take place without cause.

12.   In those days shall the mouth of hell be opened, into which they shall be immerged; hell shall destroy and swallow up sinners from the face of the elect.

CHAP. LV.

1. After this I beheld another army of chariots, with men riding in them.

2. And they came upon the wind from the east, from the west, and from the south.[116]

3. The sound of the noise of their chariots was heard.

4. And when that agitation took place, the saints out of heaven perceived it; the pillar of the earth shook from its foundation; and the sound was heard from the extremities of the earth unto the extremities of heaven at the same time.

5. Then they all fell down, and worshipped the Lord of spirits.

6. This is the end of the second parable.

---

[116] *from the midst of the day.* The army alluded to was probably Roman.

CHAP. LVI. [SECT. IX.[117]]

1. I now began to utter the third parable, concerning the saints and the elect.

2. Blessed are ye, O saints and elect, for glorious is your lot.

3. The saints shall exist in the light of the sun, and the elect in the light of everlasting life, the days of whose life shall never terminate; nor shall the days of the saints be numbered, who seek for light, and obtain righteousness with the Lord of spirits.

4. Peace be to the saints with the Lord of the world.

5. Henceforward shall the saints be told to seek in heaven the secrets of righteousness, the portion of faith; for like the sun has it arisen upon the earth, while darkness has passed away. There shall be light interminable:[118] nor shall they enter upon the enumeration of time; for darkness shall be previously destroyed, and light shall increase before the Lord of spirits; before the Lord of spirits shall the light of uprightness increase for ever.

CHAP. LVII.

1. In those days my eyes beheld the secrets of the lightnings and the splendours, and the judgment belonging to them.

2. They lighten for a blessing and for a curse, according to the will of the Lord of spirits.

3. And there I saw the secrets of the thunder, when it rattles[119] above in heaven, and its sound is heard.

4. The habitations also of the earth were shown to me. The sound of the thunder is for peace and for blessing, as well as for a curse, according to the word of the Lord of spirits.

[117] Paris MS.
[118] *which cannot be numbered.*
[119] *it is grinding, as in a mortar.*

5. Afterwards every secret of the splendours and of the lightnings was seen by me. For blessing and for fertility they lighten.

CHAP. LVIII.[120] [SECT. X.[121]]

1. In the five hundredth year, and in the seventh month, on the fourteenth *day* of the month, of the lifetime of Enoch, in that parable, I saw that the heaven of heavens shook; that it shook violently; and that the powers of the Most High, and the angels, thousands of thousands, and myriads of myriads, were agitated with great agitation. And when I looked, the Ancient of days was sitting on the throne of his glory, while the angels and saints were standing around him. A great trembling came upon me, and terror seized me. My loins were bowed down and loosened; my reins were dissolved; and I fell upon my face. The holy Michael, another holy angel, one of the holy ones, was sent, who raised me up.

2. And when he raised me, my spirit returned; for I was incapable of enduring this vision of violence, its agitation, and the concussion of heaven.

3. Then holy Michael said to me, Wherefore art thou disturbed at this vision?

4. Hitherto has existed the day of mercy; and he has been merciful and longsuffering towards all who dwell upon the earth.

5. But when the time shall come, then *shall* the power, the punishment, and the judgment take place, which the Lord of spirits has prepared for those who prostrate themselves to the judgment of righteousness, for those who abjure that judgment, and for those who take *his* name in vain.

6. That day has been prepared for the elect *as a day of* covenant; and for sinners *as a day of* inquisition.

---

[120] There is no chap. lviii. in the MS. I have therefore divided chap. lix. into two parts, denominating this first part chap. lviii.
[121] Paris MS.

7. In that day shall be distributed *for food* two monsters; a female monster, whose name is Leviathan, dwelling in the depths of the sea, above the springs of waters;

S. And a male *monster*, whose name is Behemoth; which possesses, *moving* on his breast, the invisible wilderness.

9. His name was Dendayen in the east of the garden, where the elect and the righteous will dwell; where he received *it* from my ancestor, who was man, from Adam the first of men, whom the Lord of spirits made.

10. Then I asked of another angel to show me the power of those monsters, how they became separated on the same day, one *being* in the depths of the sea, and one in the dry desert.

11. And he said, Thou, son of man, art here desirous of understanding secret things.

12. [122] And the angel of peace, who was with me, said, These two monsters are by the power of God prepared to become food, that the punishment of God may not be in vain.

13. Then shall children be slain with their mothers, and sons with their fathers.

14. And when the punishment of the Lord of spirits shall continue, upon them shall it continue, that the punishment of the Lord of spirits may not take place in vain. After that, judgment shall exist with mercy and longsuffering.

CHAP. LIX.

1. Then another angel, who proceeded with me, spoke to me;

2. And showed me the first and last secrets in heaven above, and in the depths of the earth:

---

[122] These last three verses, viz. 12, 13, 14, are placed in both MSS. at the end of chap. lix.; but they so evidently belong to this account of the Leviathan and Behemoth, that I have ventured to insert them here.

3. In the extremities of heaven, and in the foundations of it, and in the receptacle of the winds.

4. *He showed me* how their spirits were divided; how they were balanced; and how both the springs and the winds were numbered according to the force of their spirit.

5. *He showed me* the power of the moon's light, that its power is a just one; as well as the divisions of the stars, according to their respective names;

6. *That* every division is divided; that the lightning flashes;

7. That its troops[123] immediately obey; and that a cessation takes place during thunder in continuance of its sound. Nor are the thunder and the lightning separated; neither do both of them move with one spirit; yet are they not separated.

8. For when the lightning lightens, the thunder sounds, and the spirit at a proper period pauses, making an equal division between them; for the receptacle, upon which their periods depend, is *loose* as sand.[124] Each of them at a proper season is restrained with a bridle; and turned by the power of the spirit, which thus propels *them* according to the spacious extent of the earth.

9. The spirit likewise of the sea is potent and strong; and as a strong power causes it to ebb,[125] so is it driven forwards, and scattered against the mountains of the earth. The spirit of the frost has its angel; in the spirit of hail there is a good angel; the spirit of snow ceases in its strength, and a solitary spirit is in it, which ascends from it like vapour, and is called refrigeration.

10. The spirit also of mist dwells with them in their receptacle; but it has a receptacle to itself; for its progress is in splendour,

11. In light, and in darkness, in winter and in summer. It receptacle is bright, and an angel is *in it*.

---

[123] *Their host.*
[124] *the receptacle of their times is what sand is.*
[125] *turns it back with a bridle.*

12.   The spirit of dew *has* its abode in the extremities of heaven, in connection with the receptacle of rain; and its progress is in winter and in summer. The cloud produced by it, and the cloud of the mist, become united; one gives to the other; and when the spirit of rain is in motion from its receptacle, angels come, and opening its receptacle, bring it forth.

13.   When likewise it is sprinkled over all the earth, it forms an union with every kind of water on the ground; for the waters remain on the ground, because *they afford* nourishment to the earth from the Most High, who is in heaven.

14.   Upon this account therefore there is a regulation in the quantity of rain,[126] which the angels receive.

15. These things I saw; all of them, even paradise.[127]

CHAP. LX.

1. In those days I beheld long ropes given to those angels; who took to their wings, and fled, advancing towards the north.

2. And I inquired of the angel, saying, Wherefore have they taken those long ropes, and gone forth? He said, They are gone forth to measure.

3. The angel, who proceeded with me, said, These are the measures of the righteous; and cords shall the righteous bring, that they may trust in[128] the name of the Lord of spirits for ever and ever.

4. The elect shall begin to dwell with the elect.

5. And these are the measures which shall be given to faith, and *which* shall strengthen the words of righteousness.

6. These measures shall reveal all the secrets in the depth of the earth.

7. And *it shall be*, that those who have been destroyed in the desert, and who have been devoured by the fish of the sea, and by wild beasts, shall

---

[126] *a measure in the rain.*
[127] *even to the garden of the righteous.*
[128] *lean upon.*

return, and trust in 1 the day of the Elect One; for none shall perish in the presence of the Lord of spirits, nor shall any be capable of perishing.

8. Then they received the commandment, all *who were* in the heavens above; to whom a combined power, voice, and splendour, like fire, were given.

9. And first, with *their* voice, they blessed him, they exalted him, they glorified him with wisdom, and ascribed to him wisdom with the word, and with the breath of life.

10.   Then the Lord of spirits seated upon the throne of his glory the Elect One;

11.   Who shall judge all the works of the holy, in heaven above, and in a balance shall he weigh their actions. And when he shall lift up his countenance to judge their secret ways in the word of the name of the Lord of spirits, and their progress in the path of the righteous judgment of God most high;

12.   They shall all speak with united voice; and bless, glorify, exalt, and praise, in the name of the Lord of spirits.

13.   He shall call to every power of the heavens, to all the holy above, and to the power of God. The Cherubim, the Seraphim, and the Ophanin, all the angels of power, and all the angels of the Lords, namely, of the Elect One, and of the other Power, who was upon earth over the water on that day,

14.   Shall raise their united voice; shall bless, glorify, praise, and exalt with the spirit of faith, with the spirit of wisdom and patience, with the spirit of mercy, with the spirit of judgment and peace, and with the spirit of benevolence; all shall say with united voice: Blessed is He; and the name of the Lord of spirits shall be blessed for ever and for ever; all, who sleep not, shall bless it in heaven above.

15.   All the holy in heaven shall bless it; all the elect who dwell in the garden of life; and every spirit of light, who is capable of blessing, glorifying, exalting, and praising thy holy name; and every mortal

man,[129] more than the powers *of heaven*, shall glorify and bless thy name for ever and ever.

16.   For great is the mercy of the Lord of spirits; long-suffering is he; and all his works, all his power, great as are the things which he has done, has he revealed to the saints and to the elect, in the name of the Lord of spirits.

---

[129] *all of flesh.*

Chapters LXI-LXXX

CHAP. LXI.

1. Thus the Lord commanded the kings, the princes, the exalted, and those who dwell on earth, saying, Open your eyes, and lift up your horns, if you are capable of comprehending the Elect One.

2. The Lord of spirits sat upon the throne of his glory.

3. And the spirit of righteousness was poured out over him.

4. The word of his mouth shall destroy all the sinners and all the ungodly, who shall perish at his presence.

5. In that day shall all the kings, the princes, the exalted, and those who possess the earth, stand up, behold, and perceive, that he is sitting on the throne of his glory; that before him the saints shall be judged in righteousness;

6. And that nothing, which shall be spoken before him, shall be *spoken* in vain.

7. Trouble shall come upon them, as upon a woman in travail, whose labour is severe, when her child comes to the mouth of the womb, and she finds it difficult to bring forth.

8. One portion of them shall look upon another. They shall be astonished, and shall humble their countenance;

9. And trouble shall seize them, when they shall behold this Son of woman sitting upon the throne of his glory.

10. Then shall the kings, the princes, and all who possess the earth, glorify him who has dominion over all things, him who was concealed; for from the beginning the Son of man existed in secret,[130] whom the Most High preserved in the presence of his power, and revealed to the elect.

---

[130] *was concealed.*

11. He shall sow the congregation of the saints, and of the elect; and all the elect shall stand before him in that day.

12. All the kings, the princes, the exalted, and those who rule over the earth, shall fall down on their faces before him, and shall worship him.

13. They shall fix their hopes on this Son of man, shall pray to him, and petition him for mercy.

14. Then shall the Lord of spirits hasten to expel them from his presence. Their faces shall be full of confusion, and their faces shall darkness cover.[131] The angels shall take them to punishment, that vengeance may be inflicted on those who have oppressed his children and his elect. And they shall become an example to the saints and to his elect. Through them shall these be made joyful; for the anger of the Lord of spirits shall rest upon them.

15. Then the sword of the Lord of spirits shall be drunk with their blood;[132] but the saints and elect shall be safe in that day; nor the face of the sinners and the ungodly shall they thenceforwards behold.

16. The Lord of spirits shall remain over them:

17. And with this Son of man shall they dwell, eat, lie down, and rise up, for ever and ever.

18. The saints and the elect have arisen from the earth, have left off to depress their countenances, and have been clothed with the garment of life. That garment of life is with the Lord of spirits, in whose presence your garment shall not wax old, nor shall your glory diminish.

CHAP. LXII.

1. In those days the kings who possess the earth shall be punished by the angels of his wrath,[133] wheresoever they shall be delivered up, that he may give rest for a short period; and that they may fall down and worship before the Lord of spirits, confessing their sins before him.

---

[131] *be added to their faces.*
[132] *be drunk from them.*
[133] *punishment.*

2. They shall bless and glorify the Lord of spirits, saying, Blessed is the Lord of spirits, the Lord of kings, the Lord of princes, the Lord of the rich, the Lord of glory, and the Lord of wisdom.

3. He shall enlighten every secret thing.

4. Thy power is from generation to generation; and thy glory for ever and ever.

5. Deep are all thy secrets, and numberless; and thy righteousness cannot be computed.

6. Now we know, that we should glorify and bless the Lord of kings, him who is King over all things.

7. They shall also say, Who has granted us rest to glorify, laud, bless, and confess in the presence of his glory?

8. And now small is the rest we desire; but we do not find *it;* we reject, and do not possess it. Light has passed away from before us; and darkness *has covered* our thrones for ever.

9. For we have not confessed before him; we have not glorified the name of the Lord of kings; we have not glorified the Lord in all his works; but we have trusted in the sceptre of our dominion and of our glory.

10. In the day of our suffering and of our trouble he will not save us, neither shall we find rest. We confess that our Lord is faithful in all his works, in all his judgments, and in his righteousness.

11. In his judgments he pays no respect to persons; and we must depart from his presence, on account of our *evil* deeds.

12. All our sins are truly without number.

13. Then shall they say to themselves, Our souls are satiated with the instruments of crime;

14. But that prevents us not from descending to the flaming womb of hell.

15. Afterwards, their countenances shall be filled with darkness and confusion before the Son of man; from whose presence they shall be expelled, and before whom the sword shall remain to expel them.

16. Thus saith the Lord of spirits, This is the decree and the judgment against the princes, the kings, the exalted, and those who possess the earth, in the presence of the Lord of spirits.

CHAP. LXIII.

1. I saw also other countenances in that secret place. I heard the voice of an angel, saying, These are the angels who have descended from heaven to earth, and have revealed secrets to the sons of men, and have seduced the sons of men to the commission of sin.

CHAP. LXIV. [SECT. XI.[134]]

1. In those days Noah saw that the earth became inclined, and that destruction approached.

2. Then he lifted up his feet, and went to the ends of the earth, to the dwelling of his great-grandfather Enoch.

3. And Noah cried with a bitter voice, Hear me; hear me; hear me: three times. And he said, Tell me what is transacting upon earth; for the earth labours, and is violently shaken. Surely I shall perish with it.

4. After this there was a great perturbation on earth, and a voice was heard from heaven. I fell down on my face, when my great-grandfather Enoch came and stood by me.

5. He said to me, Why hast thou cried out to me with a bitter cry and lamentation?

6. A commandment has gone forth from the Lord against those who dwell on the earth, that they may be destroyed;[135] for they know every secret of the angels, every oppressive and secret power of the devils,[136] and every power of those who commit sorcery, as well as of those who make molten images in the whole earth.

---

[134] Chapters lxiv. lxv. lxvi. and the first verse of lxvii. evidently contain a vision of Noah, and not of Enoch.
[135] *their end may be.*
[136] *the Satans.*

7. *They know* how silver is produced from the dust of the earth, and how on the earth the *metallic* drop exists; for lead and tin are not produced from earth, as the primary fountain of their production.

8. There is an angel standing upon it, and that angel struggles to prevail.

9. Afterwards my great-grandfather Enoch seized me with his hand, raising me up, and saying to me, Go, for I have asked the Lord of spirits respecting this perturbation of the earth; who replied, On account of their impiety have their innumerable judgments been consummated before me. Respecting the moons have they inquired, and they have known that the earth will perish with those who dwell upon it, and that to these there will be no *place of* refuge for ever.

10.   They have discovered secrets, and *they are* those who have been judged; but not thou, my son. The Lord of spirits knows that thou art pure and good, *free* from the reproach of *discovering* secrets.

11.   He, the holy One, will establish thy name in the midst of the saints, and will preserve thee from those who dwell upon the earth. He will establish thy seed in righteousness, with dominion and great glory;[137] and from thy seed shall spring forth[138] righteous and holy men without number for ever.

CHAP. LXV.

1. After this he showed me the angels of punishment, who were prepared to come, and to open all the mighty waters[139] under the earth:

2. That they may be for judgment, and for the destruction of all those who remain and dwell upon the earth.

3. And the Lord of spirits commanded the angels who went forth, not to take up the men and preserve *them.*

4. For those angels *presided* over all the mighty waters. Then I went out from the presence of Enoch.

[137] *for kings, and for great glory.*
[138] *shall go forth a spring of.*
[139] *the power of water.*

CHAP. LXVI.

1. In those days the word of God came to me,[140] and said, Noah, behold, thy lot[141] has ascended up to me, a lot void of crime,[142] a lot beloved[143] and upright.

2. Now then shall the angels labour at the trees; but when they proceed to this, I will put my hand upon it, and preserve it.

3. The seed of life shall arise[144] from it, and a change shall take place,[145] that the dry land may not be left empty. I will establish thy seed before me for ever and ever, and the seed of those who dwell with thee on the surface of the earth. It shall be blessed and multiplied in the presence of the earth, in the name of the Lord.

4. And they shall confine those angels who disclosed impiety. In that burning valley *it is, that they shall be confined*, which at first my great-grandfather Enoch showed me in the west, where there were mountains of gold and silver, of iron, of fluid metal, and of tin.

5. I beheld that valley in which there was great perturbation, and *where* the waters were troubled.

6. And when all this was effected, from the fluid mass of fire, and the perturbation which prevailed[146] in that place, there arose a strong smell of sulphur, which became mixed with the waters; and the valley of the angels, who had been guilty of seduction, burned underneath its soil.

7. Through that valley also rivers of fire were flowing,[147] to which those angels shall be condemned, who seduced the inhabitants of the earth.

8. And in those days shall these waters be to kings, to princes, to the exalted, and to the inhabitants of the earth, for the healing of the soul and body, and for the judgment of the spirit.

[140] *was with me.*
[141] *portion.*
[142] *fault.*
[143] *of love.*
[144] *be.*
[145] *shall enter.*
[146] *troubled them.*
[147] *went.*

9. Their spirits shall be full of revelry,[148] that they may be judged in their bodies; because they have denied the Lord of spirits, and *although* they perceive their condemnation day by day, they believe not in his name.

10.   And as the inflammation of their bodies shall be great, so shall their spirits undergo a change for ever.

11.   For no word which is uttered before the Lord of spirits shall be in vain.

12.   Judgment has come upon them, because they trusted in their carnal revelry,[149] and denied the Lord of spirits.

13.   In those days shall the waters of that valley[150] be changed; for when the angels shall be judged, then shall the heat of those springs of water experience an alteration.

14. And when the angels shall ascend, the water of the springs shall *again* undergo a change, and be frozen. Then I heard holy Michael answering and saying, This judgment, with which the angels shall be judged, shall bear testimony against the kings, the princes, and those who possess the earth.

15.   For these waters of judgment shall be for their healing, and for the death of their bodies. But they shall not perceive and believe that the waters will be changed, and become a fire, which shall blaze for ever.

CHAP. LXVII.

1. After this he gave me the characteristical marks[151] of all the secret things in the book of my great-grandfather Enoch, and in the parables which had been given to him; inserting them for me among the words of the book of parables.

2. At that time holy Michael answered and said to Raphael, The power of the spirit hurries me away, and impels me on.[152] The severity of the

[148] *sport.*
[149] *sport of their bodies.*
[150] *its waters.*
[151] *the signs.*
[152] *irritates* or *excites me.*

judgment, of the secret judgment of the angels, who is capable *of beholding*—the endurance of that severe judgment which has taken place and been made permanent—without being melted at the sight of it?[153] Again holy Michael answered and said to holy Raphael, Who is there whose heart is not softened by it, and whose reins are not troubled at this thing?

3. Judgment has gone forth against them by those who have thus dragged them away; and that was, when they stood in the presence of the Lord of spirits.

4. In like manner also holy Rakael said to Raphael, They shall not be before the eye of the Lord; since the Lord of spirits has been offended with them; for like Lords[154] have they conducted themselves. Therefore will he bring upon them a secret judgment for ever and ever.

5. For neither shall angel nor man receive a portion of it; but they alone shall receive their own judgment for ever and ever.

CHAP. LXVIII.

1. After this judgment they shall be astonished and irritated; for it shall be exhibited to the inhabitants of the earth.

2. Behold the names of those angels. These are their names. The first of them is Samyaza; the second, Arstikapha: the third, Armen; the fourth, Kakabael; the fifth, Turel; the sixth, Rumyel; the seventh, Danyal; the eighth, Kael; the ninth, Barakel; the tenth, Azazel; the eleventh, Armers; the twelfth, Bataryal; the thirteenth, Basasael; the fourteenth, Ananel; the fifteenth, Turyal; the sixteenth, Simapiseel; the seventeenth, Yetarel; the eighteenth, Tumael; the nineteenth, Tarel; the twentieth, Rumel; the twenty-first, Azazyel.

3. These are the chiefs of their angels, and the names of the leaders of their hundreds, and the leaders of their fifties, and the leaders of their tens.

[153] *and not be melted in the presence of it.*
[154] *in the similitude of, or, as the Lord.*

4. The name of the first is Yekun: he it was who seduced all the sons of the holy angels; and causing them to descend on earth, led astray the offspring of men.

5. The name of the second is Kesabel, who pointed out evil counsel to the sons of the holy angels, and induced them to corrupt their bodies by generating mankind.

6. The name of the third is Gadrel: he discovered every stroke of death to the children of men.

7. He seduced Eve; and discovered to the children of men the instruments of death, the coat of mail, the shield, and the sword for slaughter; every instrument of death to the children of men.

8. From his hand were these things derived to them who dwell upon earth, from that period for ever.

9. The name of the fourth is Penemue: he discovered to the children of men bitterness and sweetness;

10. And pointed out to them every secret of their wisdom.

11. He taught men to understand writing, and the use of f ink and paper.

12. Therefore numerous have been those who have gone astray from every period of the world, even to this day.

13. For men were not born for this, thus with pen and with ink to confirm their faith;

14. Since they were not created, except that, like the angels, they might remain righteous and pure.

15. Nor would death, which destroys everything, have affected them;

16. But by this their knowledge they perish, and by this also *its* power consumes[155] *them*.

17. The name of the fifth is Kasyade: he discovered to the children of men every wicked stroke of spirits and of demons:

[155] *eats, feeds upon, devours.*

18. The stroke of the embryo in the womb, to diminish *it;* the stroke of the spirit *by* the bite of the serpent, and the stroke which is *given* in the mid-day *by* the offspring of the serpent, the name of which is Tabaet.[156]

19. This is the number of the Kesbel; the principal part of the oath which the Most High, dwelling in glory, revealed to the holy ones.

20. Its name is Beka. He spoke to holy Michael to discover to them the sacred name, that they might understand that secret name, and thus remember the oath; and that those who pointed out every secret thing to the children of men might tremble at that name and oath.

21. This is the power of that oath; for powerful it is, and strong.

22. And he established this oath of Akae by the instrumentality[157] of the holy Michael.

23. These are the secrets of this oath, and by it were they confirmed.

24. Heaven was suspended *by it* before the world was made, for ever.

25. By it has the earth been founded upon the flood; while from the concealed parts of the hills the agitated waters proceed forth from the creation to the end of the world.

26. By this oath the sea has been formed, and the foundation of it.

27. During the period of *its* fury he has established the sand against it, which continues unchanged for ever; and by this oath the abyss has been made strong; nor is it removable from its station for ever and ever.

28. By this oath the sun and moon complete their progress, never swerving from the command *given* to them for ever and ever.

29. By this oath the stars complete their progress;

30. And when their names are called, they return an answer, for ever and ever.

31. Thus *in* the heavens *take place* the blowings of the winds: all of them have breathings,[158] and *effect* a complete combination of breathings.

---

[156] *male.*
[157] *by the hands.*

32. There the treasures of thunder are kept, and the splendour of the lightning.

33. There are kept the treasures of hail and of frost, the treasures of snow, the treasures of rain and of dew.

34. All these confess and laud before the Lord of spirits.

35. They glorify with all their power of praise; and he sustains them in all that *act of* thanksgiving; while they laud, glorify, and exalt the name of the Lord of spirits for ever and ever.

36. And with them he establishes this oath, by which they and their paths are preserved; nor does their progress perish.

37. Great was their joy.

38. They blessed, glorified, and exalted, because the name of the Son of man was revealed to them.

39. He sat upon the throne of his glory; and the principal part of the judgment was assigned to him, the Son of man. Sinners shall disappear and perish from the face of the earth, while those who seduced them shall be bound with chains for ever.

40. According to their ranks of corruption shall they be imprisoned, and all their works shall disappear from the face of the earth; nor thenceforward shall there be any to corrupt; for the Son of man has been seen, sitting on the throne of his glory.

41. Everything wicked shall disappear, and depart from before his face; and the word of the Son of man shall become powerful in the presence of the Lord of spirits.

42. This is the third parable of Enoch.

CHAP. LXIX. [SECT. XII.[159]]

1. After this the name of the Son of man, living with the Lord of spirits,[160] was exalted by the inhabitants of the earth.

[158] or *spirits.*
[159] Paris MS.

2. It was exalted in the chariots of the Spirit; and the name went forth in the midst of them.

3. From that time I was not drawn in the midst of them; but he seated me between two spirits, between the north and the west, where the angels received their ropes, to measure out a place[161] for the elect and the righteous.

4. There I beheld the fathers of the first men, and the saints, who dwell in that place for ever.

CHAP. LXX.

1. Afterwards my spirit was concealed, ascending into the heavens. I beheld the sons of the holy angels treading on flaming fire, whose garments and robes were white, and whose countenances were transparent as crystal.

2. I saw two rivers of fire glittering like the hyacinth,

3. Then I fell on my face before the Lord of spirits.

4. And Michael, one of the archangels, took me by my right hand, raised me up, and brought me out *to* where was every secret *of* mercy and secret *of* righteousness.

5. He showed me all the hidden things of the extremities of heaven, all the receptacles of the stars, and the splendours of all, from whence they went forth before the face of the holy.

6. And he concealed the spirit of Enoch in the heaven of heavens.

7. There I beheld, in the midst of that light, a building raised with stones of ice;[162]

8. And in the midst of these stones vibrations[163] of living fire. My spirit saw around the circle of[164] this flaming habitation, on one of its

---

[160] *the name of him living with him, of this Son of man, living with the Lord of spirits.*
[161] *to measure me a place.*
[162] *that in it there was that which was built with stones of ice.*
[163] *tongues.*
[164] *around that which encompassed.*

extremities, *that there were* rivers full of living fire, which encompassed it.

9. Then the Seraphim, the Cherubim, and Ophanin surrounded *it* these are those who never sleep, but watch the throne of his glory.

10. And I beheld angels innumerable, thousands of thousands, and myriads of myriads, who surrounded that habitation.

11. Michael, Raphael, Gabriel, Phanuel, and the holy angels who were in the heavens above, went in and out of it. Michael, Raphael, and Gabriel went out of that habitation, and holy angels innumerable.

12. With them *was* the Ancient of days, whose head *was* white as wool, and pure, and his robe was indescribable.

13. Then I fell upon my face, while all my flesh was dissolved, and my spirit became changed.

14. I cried out with a loud voice, with a powerful spirit, blessing, glorifying, and exalting.

15. And those blessings, which proceeded from my mouth, became acceptable in the presence of the Ancient of days.

16. The Ancient of days came with Michael and Gabriel, Raphael and Phanuel, with thousands of thousands, and myriads of myriads, which could not be numbered.

17. Then that angel came to me, and with his voice saluted me, saying, Thou art the offspring of man, who art born for righteousness, and righteousness has rested on thee.

18. The righteousness of the Ancient of days shall not forsake thee.

19. He said, On thee shall he confer peace[165] in the name of the existing world; for from thence has peace gone forth since the world was created.

20. And thus shall it happen to thee for ever and ever.

21. All who shall exist, and who shall walk in thy path of righteousness, shall not forsake thee for ever.

[165] *he shall call to thee peace.*

22.   With thee shall be their habitations, with thee their lot; nor from thee shall they be separated for ever and ever.

23. And thus shall length of days be with the offspring of man.

24.   Peace shall be to the righteous; and the path of integrity shall the righteous pursue,[166] in the name of the Lord of spirits, for ever and ever.

CHAP. LXXI. [SECT. XIII.[167]]

1. The book of the revolutions of the luminaries of heaven, according to their respective classes, their respective powers, their respective periods, their respective names, the places where they commence their progress,[168] and their respective months, which Uriel, the holy angel who was with me, explained to me; he who conducts them. The whole account of them, according to every year of the world for ever, until a new work shall be effected, which will be eternal.

2. This is the first law of the luminaries. The sun *and* the light arrive at the gates of heaven, which are on the east, and on the west of it at the western gates of heaven.

3. I beheld the gates whence the sun goes forth; and the gates where the sun sets;

4. In which gates also the moon rises and sets; and *I beheld* the conductors of the stars, among those who precede them; six *gates were* at the rising, and six at the setting of the sun.

5. All these respectively, one after another, are on a level; and numerous windows are on the right and on the left sides of those gates.

6. First proceeds forth that great luminary, which is called the sun; the orb of which is as the orb of heaven, the whole of it being replete with splendid and flaming fire.

7. Its chariot, where it ascends, the wind blows.

---

[166] *his upright path shall be to the righteous.*
[167] Paris MS.
[168] *the places of their nativity.*

8. The sun sets in heaven, and, returning by the north, to proceed towards the east, is conducted so as to enter by that gate, and illuminate the face of heaven.

9. In the same manner it goes forth in the first month by a great gate.

10. It goes forth through the fourth of those six gates, which are at the rising of the sun.

11. And in the fourth gate, through which the sun with the moon proceeds, in the first part of it, there are twelve open windows; from which issues out a flame, when they are opened at their proper periods.

12. When the sun rises in heaven, it goes forth through this fourth gate thirty days, and by the fourth gate in the west of heaven on a level with it descends.

13. During that period the day is lengthened from the day, and the night curtailed from the night for thirty days. And then the day is longer by two parts than the night.

14. The day is precisely ten parts, and the night is eight.

15. The sun[169] goes forth through this fourth gate, and sets in it, and turns to the fifth gate during thirty days; after which it proceeds from, and sets in, the fifth gate.

16. Then the day becomes lengthened by a second portion, so that it is eleven parts: while the night becomes shortened, and is only seven parts.

17. The sun *now* returns to the east, entering into the sixth gate, and rising and setting in the sixth gate thirty-one days, on account of its signs.

18. At that period the day is longer than the night, being twice *as long as* the night; and becomes twelve parts;

19. But the night is shortened, and becomes six parts. Then the sun rises up, that the day may be shortened, and the night lengthened.

20. And the sun returns towards the east, entering into the sixth gate, where it rises and sets for thirty days.

[169] *And he.*

21.   When that period is completed, the day becomes shortened precisely one part, so that it is eleven parts, while the night is seven parts.

22.   Then the sun goes from the west, from that sixth gate, and proceeds eastwards, rising in the fifth gate for thirty days, and setting again westwards in the fifth gate of the west.

23.   At that period the day becomes shortened two parts; and is ten parts, while the night is eight parts.

24.   Then the sun goes from the fifth gate, as it sets in the fifth gate of the west; and rises in the fourth gate for thirty-one days, on account of its signs, setting in the west.

25.   At that period the day is made equal with the night; and, being equal with it, the night becomes nine parts, and the day nine parts.

26.   Then the sun goes from that gate, as it sets in the west; and returning to the east proceeds by the third gate for thirty days, setting in the west at the third gate.

27.   At that period the night is lengthened from the day during thirty mornings, and the day is curtailed from the day during thirty days; the night being ten parts precisely, and the day eight parts.

28.   The sun now goes from the third gate, as it sets in the third gate in the west; but returning to the east, it proceeds by the second gate of the east for thirty days.

29. In like manner also it sets in the second gate in the west of heaven.

30. At that period the night is eleven parts, and the day seven parts.

31.   Then the sun goes at that time from the second gate, as it sets in the second gate in the west; but returns to the east, *proceeding* by the first gate, for thirty-one days.

32. And sets in the west in the first[170] gate.

33. At that period the night is lengthened as much again as the day.

34. It is twelve[171] parts precisely, while the day is six parts.

---

[170] *second*. A manifest error. The Paris MS. is correct.

35.   The sun has *thus* completed its beginnings, and a second time goes round from these beginnings.

36.   Into that gate it enters for thirty days, and sets in the west, in the opposite part *of heaven.*

37.   At that period the night is contracted in its length a fourth part, that is, one portion, and becomes eleven parts.

38. The day is seven parts.

39. Then the sun returns, and enters into the second gate of the east.

40. It returns by these beginnings thirty days, rising and setting.

41. At that period the night is contracted in its length. It becomes ten[172] parts, and the day eight parts. Then the sun goes from that second gate, and sets in the west; but returns to the east, and rises in the east, in the third gate, thirty-one days, setting in the west of heaven.

42.   At that period the night becomes shortened. It is nine parts. And the night is equal with the day. The year is precisely three hundred and sixty-four days.

43.   The lengthening of the day and night, and the contraction of the day and night, are made to differ from each other by the progress of the sun.

44.   By means of this progress the day is daily lengthened, and the night greatly shortened.[173]

45.   This is the law and progress of the sun, and its turning when it turns back, turning during sixty days,[174] and going forth. This is the great everlasting luminary, that which he names the sun for ever and ever.

46.   This also is that which goes forth a great luminary, and which is named after its peculiar kind, as God commanded.

47.   And thus it goes in and out, neither slackening nor resting; but running on in its chariot by day and by night. It shines with a seventh portion of light from the moon; but the dimensions of both are equal.

[171] *eleven.* A mistake of the transcriber. In the Paris MS. it is *twelve.*
[172] *seven.* Another error.
[173] *approaches.*
[174] That is, it is sixty days in the same gates, viz. thirty days twice every year.

CHAP. LXXII. [SECT. XIV.[175]]

1. After this law I beheld another law of an inferior luminary, the name of which is the moon, and the orb of which is as the orb of heaven.

2. Its chariot, *which* it secretly ascends, the wind blows; and light is given to it by measure.

3. Every month at its exit and entrance it becomes changed; and its periods are as the periods of the sun. And when in like manner its light is to exist, its light is a seventh portion from the light of the sun.

4. Thus it rises, and at its commencement towards the east goes forth for thirty days.

5. At that time it appears, and becomes to you the beginning of the month. Thirty days *it is* with the sun in the gate from which the sun goes forth.

6. Half of it is in extent seven portions, one *half;* and the whole of its orb is void of light, except a seventh portion out of the fourteen portions of its light. And in a day it receives a seventh portion, or half *that portion*, of its light. Its light is by sevens, by one portion, and by the half *of a portion*. It sets with the sun.

7. And when the sun rises, the moon rises with it; receiving half a portion of light.

8. On that night, when it commences its period,[176] previously to the day of the month, the moon sets with the sun.

9. And on that night it is dark *in* its fourteen portions, that is, *in each* half; but it rises on that day with one seventh portion precisely, and in its progress declines from the rising of the sun.

10. During the remainder of its period[177] its light increases to fourteen portions.

[175] Paris MS.
[176] *at the beginning of its morning, or day.*
[177] *of its day.*

CHAP. LXXIII.

1. Then I saw another progress and regulation which He effected in the law of the moon.[178] The progress of the moons, and everything *relating to them*, Uriel showed me, the holy angel who conducted them all.

2. Their stations I wrote down as he showed them to me.

3. I wrote down their months, as they occur, and the appearance of their light, until it is completed in fifteen days.

4. In each of its two seven portions it completes all its light at rising and at setting.

5. On stated months it changes *its* settings; and on stated months it makes its progress *through* each gate. In two *gates* the moon sets with the sun, viz. in those two gates which are in the midst, in the third and fourth gate. *From the third gate* it goes forth for seven days, and makes its circuit.

6. Again it returns to the gate whence the sun goes forth, and in that completes the whole of its light. Then it declines from the sun, and enters in eight days into the sixth gate, *and returns in seven days to the third gate*, from which the sun goes forth.

7. When the sun proceeds to the fourth gate, the *moon* goes forth for seven days, until it passes from the fifth *gate*.

8. Again it returns in seven days to the fourth gate, and completing all its light, declines, and passes on by the first gate in eight days;

9. And returns in seven days to the fourth gate, from which the sun goes forth.

10. Thus I beheld their stations, as according to the fixed order of the months the sun rises and sets.

11. At those times there is an excess of thirty days belonging to the sun in five years; all the days belonging to each year of the five years, when completed, amount to three hundred and sixty-four days; and to the sun

[178] *in that law.*

and stars belong six days; six days in each of the five years; *thus* thirty days belong to them;

12. So that the moon has thirty days less than the sun and stars.

13.　The moon brings on all the years exactly, that their stations may come neither too forwards nor too backwards a single day; but that the years may be changed with correct precision in three hundred and sixty-four days. In three years the days are one thousand and ninety-two; in five years they are one thousand eight hundred and twenty; and in eight years two thousand nine hundred and twelve days.

14.　To the moon alone belong in three years one thousand and sixty-two days; in five years it has fifty days less *than the sun*, for an addition being made to the *one thousand and* sixty-two days, in five years there are one thousand seven hundred and seventy days; and the days of the moon in eight years are two thousand eight hundred and thirty-two days.

15.　For its days in eight years are less *than those of the sun by* eighty days, which eighty days are its diminution in eight years.

16.　The year then becomes truly complete according to the station of the moons, and the station of the sun; which rise in the *different* gates; which rise and set in them for thirty days.

CHAP. LXXIV.

1. *These are* the leaders of the chiefs of the
thousands, *those* which *preside* over all creation, and over all the stars; with the four *days* which are added and never separated from the place allotted them, according to the complete computation of the year.

2. And these serve four days, which are not computed in the computation of the year.

3. Respecting them, men greatly err, for these luminaries truly serve, in the mansion of the world, one *day* in the first gate, one in the third gate, one in the fourth, and one in the sixth gate.

4. And the harmony of the world becomes complete every three hundred and sixty-fourth state of it. For the signs,

5. The seasons,

6. The years,

7. And the days, Uriel showed me; the angel whom the Lord of glory appointed over all the luminaries.

8. Of heaven in heaven, and in the world; that they might rule in the face of the sky, and appearing over the earth, become

9. Conductors of the days and nights: the sun, the moon, the stars, and all the ministers of heaven, which make their circuit with all the chariots of heaven.

10. Thus Uriel showed me twelve gates open for the circuit of the chariots of the sun in heaven, from which the rays of the sun shoot forth.

11. From these proceed heat over the earth, when they are opened in their stated seasons. They are for the winds, and the spirit of the dew, when in their seasons they are opened; opened in heaven at *its* extremities.

12. Twelve gates I beheld in heaven, at the extremities of the earth, through which the sun, moon, and stars, and all the works of heaven, proceed at their rising and setting.

13. Many windows also are open on the right and on the left.

14. One window at a *certain* season grows extremely hot. So also are there gates from which the stars go forth as they are commanded, and in which they set according to their number.

15. I saw likewise the chariots of heaven, running in the world above to those gates in which the stars turn, which never set. One of these is greater than all, which goes round the whole world.

CHAP. LXXV. [SECT. XV.[179]]

1. And at the extremities of the earth I beheld twelve gates open for all the winds, from which they proceed and blow over the earth.

[179] Paris MS.

2. Three of them are open in the front of heaven, three in the west, three on the right side of heaven, and three on the left. The first three are those which are towards the east, three are towards the north, three behind those which are upon the left, towards the south, and three on the west.

3. From four of them proceed winds of blessing, and of health; and from eight proceed winds of punishment; when they are sent to destroy the earth, and the heaven above it, all its inhabitants, and all which are in the waters, or on dry land.

4. The first of these winds proceeds from the gate termed the eastern, through the first gate on the east, which inclines southwards. From this goes forth destruction, drought, heat, and perdition.

5. From the second gate, the middle one, proceeds equity. There issue from it rain, fruitfulness, health, and dew; and from the third gate northwards, proceed cold and drought.

6. After these proceed the south winds through three principal gates; through their first gate, which inclines eastwards, proceeds a hot wind.

7. But from the middle gate proceed grateful odour, dew, rain, health, and life.

8. From the third gate, which is westwards, proceed dew, rain, blight, and destruction.

9. After these are the winds to the north, which is called the sea. *They proceed* from three gates. The first[180] gate *is that* which is on the east, inclining southwards; from this proceed dew, rain, blight, and destruction. From the middle direct gate proceed rain, dew, life, and health. And from the third gate, which is westwards, inclining towards the south,[181] proceed mist, frost, snow, rain, dew, and blight.

10.   After these *in the* fourth *quarter* are the winds to the west. From the first gate, inclining northwards, proceed dew, rain, frost, cold, snow, and chill; from the middle gate proceed rain, health, and blessing;

11.   And from the last gate, which is southwards, proceed drought, destruction, scorching, and perdition.

[180] *seventh.* Perhaps the seventh which had been enumerated.
[181] *the north.* An error in both MSS.

12.   The *account of the* twelve gates of the four quarters of heaven is ended.

13. All their laws, all their *infliction* of punishment, and the health *produced* by them, have I explained to thee, my son Mathusala.

CHAP. LXXVI.

1. The first wind is called the eastern, because it is the first.

2. The second is called the south, because the Most High there descends, and frequently there descends *he who* is blessed for ever.

3. The western wind has the name of diminution, because there all the luminaries of heaven are diminished, and descend.

4. The fourth wind, which is named the north, is divided into three parts; one of which is for the habitation of man; another for seas of water, with valleys, woods, rivers, shady places, and snow; and the third part *contains* paradise.

5. Seven high mountains I beheld, higher than all the mountains of the earth, from which frost proceeds; while days, seasons, and years depart and pass away.

6. Seven rivers I beheld upon earth, greater than all rivers, one of which takes its course from the west; into a great sea its water flows.

7. Two come from the north to the sea, their waters flowing into the Erythræan sea, on the east. And with respect to the remaining four, they take their course in the cavity of the north, *two* to their sea, the Erythræan sea, and two are poured into a great sea, where also it is said *there is* a desert.

8. Seven great islands I saw in the sea and on the earth. Seven in the great sea.

CHAP. LXXVII.

1. The names of the sun are these: one Aryares, the other Tomas.

2. The moon has four names. The first is Asonya; the second, Ebla; the third, Benase; and the fourth, Erae.

3. These are the two great luminaries, whose orbs are as the orbs of heaven; and the dimensions of both are equal.

4. In the orb of the sun *there is* a seventh portion of light, which is added to it from the moon. By measure it is put in, until a seventh portion of *the light of* the sun is departed. They set, enter into the western gate, circuit by the north, and through the eastern gate go forth over the face of heaven.

5. When the moon rises, it appears in heaven; and the half of a seventh portion of light is all *which is* in it.

6. In fourteen *days* the whole of its light is completed.

7. *By* three quintuples light is put into it, until *in* fifteen *days* its light is completed, according to the signs of the year; it has three quintuples.

8. The moon has the half of a seventh portion.

9. During its diminution on the first day its light decreases a fourteenth part; on the second day it decreases a thirteenth part; on the third day a twelfth part; on the fourth day an eleventh part; on the fifth day a tenth part; on the sixth day a ninth part; on the seventh day it decreases an eighth part; on the eighth day it decreases a seventh part; on the ninth day it decreases a sixth part; on the tenth day it decreases a fifth part; on the eleventh day it decreases a fourth part; on the twelfth day it decreases a third part; on the thirteenth day it decreases a second part; on the fourteenth day it decreases a half of its seventh part; and on the fifteenth day the whole remainder of its light is consumed.

10. On stated months the moon has twenty-nine days.

11. It also has a period of twenty-eight days.

12. Uriel likewise showed me another regulation, when light is poured into the moon, how it is poured into it from the sun.

13. All the time that the moon is in progress with its light, it is poured *into it* in the presence of the sun, until *its* light is in fourteen days completed in heaven.

14. And when it is wholly extinguished, its light is consumed in heaven; and on the first day it is called the new moon, for on that day light is received into it.

15. It becomes precisely completed on the day that the sun descends into the west, while the moon ascends at night from the east.

16. The moon then shines all the night, until the sun rises before it; when the moon disappears in turn before the sun.

17. Where light comes to the moon, there again it decreases, until all its light is extinguished, and the days of the moon pass away.

18. Then its orb remains solitary without light.

19. During three months it effects in thirty days *each month* its period; and during three *more* months it effects it in twenty-nine days each. *These are the times* in which it effects its decrease in its first period, and in the first gate, *namely*, in one hundred and seventy-seven days.

20. And at the time of its going forth during three months it appears thirty days each, and during three *more* months it appears twenty-nine days each.

21. In the night it appears for each twenty *days* as *the face of* a man, and in the day as heaven; for it is nothing else except its light.

CHAP. LXXVIII.

1. And now, my son Mathusala, I have shown thee everything; and *the account of* every ordinance of the stars of heaven is finished.

2. He showed me every ordinance respecting these, which *takes place* at all times and in all seasons under every influence, in all years, at the arrival and under the rule of each, during every month and every week. *He showed me* also the decrease of the moon, which is effected in the sixth gate; for in that sixth gate is its light consumed.

3. From this is the beginning of the month; and its decrease is effected in the sixth gate in its period, until a hundred and seventy-seven days are

completed; according to the mode of computation by weeks,[182] twenty-five *weeks* and two days.

4. *Its period* is less than that of the sun, according to the ordinance of the stars, by five days in one half year[183] precisely.

5. When that *their* visible situation is completed. Such is the appearance and likeness of every luminary, which Thiel, the great angel who conducts them, showed to me.

CHAP. LXXIX.

1. In those days Uriel answered and said to me, Behold, I have showed thee all things, O Enoch;

2. And all things have I revealed to thee. Thou seest the sun, the moon, and those which conduct the stars of heaven, which cause all their operations, seasons, and arrivals to return.

3. In the days of sinners the years shall be shortened.

4. Their seed shall be backward in their prolific soil; and everything done on earth shall be subverted, and disappear in its season. The rain shall be restrained, and heaven shall stand still.

5. In those days the fruits of the earth shall be late, and not flourish in their season; and in their season the fruits of the trees shall be withholden.

6. The moon shall change its laws, and not be seen at its proper period. But in those days shall heaven be seen; and barrenness shall take place in the borders of the great chariots in the west. *Heaven* shall shine more than *when illuminated by* the orders of light; while many chiefs among the stars of authority shall err, perverting their ways and works.

7. Those shall not appear in their season, who command them, and all the classes of the stars shall be shut up against sinners.

---

[182] *according to the ordinance of the week.*
[183] *in one time.*

8. The thoughts of those who dwell on earth shall transgress within them; and they shall be perverted in all their ways.

9. They shall transgress, and think themselves gods; while evil shall be multiplied among them.

10.   And punishment shall come upon them, so that all of them shall be destroyed.

CHAP. LXXX.

1. He said, O Enoch, look on the book which heaven has gradually dropped down;[184] and, reading that which is written in it, understand every part of it.

2. Then I looked on all which was written, and understood all, reading the book and everything written in it, all the works of man;

3. And of all the children of flesh upon earth, during the generations of the world.

4. Immediately after I blessed the Lord, the King of glory, who has thus for ever formed the whole workmanship of the world.

5. And I glorified the Lord, on account of his long-suffering and blessing towards the children of the world.

6. At that time I said, Blessed is the man, who shall die righteous and good, against whom no catalogue of crime has been written, and with whom iniquity is not found.

7. Then those three holy ones caused me to approach, and placed me on the earth, before the door of my house.

8. And they said unto me, Explain everything to Mathusala thy son; and inform all thy children, that no flesh shall be justified before the Lord; for he is their Creator.

9. During one year we will leave thee with thy children, until thou shalt again recover thy strength, that thou mayest instruct thy family, write

[184] *has distilled.*

these things, and explain them to all thy children. But in another year they shall take thee from the midst of them, and thy heart shall be strengthened; for the elect shall point out righteousness to the elect; the righteous with the righteous shall rejoice, congratulating each other; but sinners with sinners shall die,

10. And the perverted with the perverted shall be drowned.

11.   Those likewise who act righteously shall die on account of the works of man, and shall be gathered together on account of the works of the wicked.

12. In those days they finished conversing with me.

13. And I returned to my fellow men, blessing the Lord of worlds.

Chapters LXXXI-C

CHAP. LXXXI.

1. Now, my son Mathusala, all these things I speak unto thee, and write for thee. To thee I have revealed all, and have given thee books of everything.

2. Preserve, my son Mathusala, the books written by thy father;[185] that thou mayest transmit them to future generations.

3. Wisdom have I given to thee, to thy children, and thy posterity, that they may transmit to their children, for generations for ever, this wisdom in their thoughts; and that those who comprehend it may not slumber, but hear with their ears; that they may learn this wisdom, and be deemed worthy of eating *this* wholesome food.

4. Blessed are all the righteous; blessed all who walk in *the paths of* righteousness; in whom no crime *is found*, as in sinners, when all their days are numbered.

5. With respect to the progress of the sun in heaven, it enters and goes out of each gate for thirty days, with the leaders of the thousand classes of the stars; with four which are added, and appertain to the four quarters of the year, which conduct them, and accompany them at four periods.

6. Respecting these, men greatly err, and do not compute them in the computation of every age; for they greatly err respecting them; nor do men know accurately that they are in the computation of the year. But indeed these are marked down[186] for ever; one in the first gate, one in the third, one in the fourth, and one in the sixth:

7. So that the year is completed in three hundred and sixty-four days.

8. Truly has been stated,[187] and accurately has been computed that which is marked down; for the luminaries, the months, the fixed periods, the

---

[185] *the books of the hand of thy father.*
[186] *to impress, express, or to seal.*
[187] *have they related.*

years, and the days, Uriel has explained to me, and communicated to me;[188] whom the Lord of all creation, on my account, commanded (according to the might of heaven, and the power which it possesses both by night and by day) to explain *the laws of* light to man, of the sun, moon, and stars, and of all the powers of heaven, which are turned with their respective orbs.

9. This is the ordinance of the stars, which set in their places, in their seasons, in their periods, in their days, and in their months.

10. These are the names of those who conduct them, who watch and enter in their seasons, according to their ordinance in their periods, in their months, in *the times of* their influence, and in their stations.

11. Four conductors of them first enter, who separate the four quarters of the year. After these, twelve conductors of their classes, who separate the months and the year *into* three hundred and sixty-four *days*, with the leaders of a thousand, who distinguish between the days, as well as between the four additional ones; which, *as* conductors, divide the four quarters of the year.

12. These leaders of a thousand are in the midst of the conductors, and the conductors are added each behind his station, and their conductors make the separation. These are the names of the conductors, who separate the four quarters of the year, who are appointed *over them:* Melkel, Helammelak,

13. Meliyal, and Narel.

14. And the names of those who conduct them are Adnarel, Jyasusal, and Jyelumeal.

15. These are the three who follow after the conductors of the classes *of stars;* each following after the three conductors of the classes, which themselves follow after those conductors of the stations, who divide the four quarters of the year.

16. In the first part of the year rises and rules Melkyas, who is named Tamani, and Zahay.[189]

---

[188] *has breathed into me.*
[189] *the sun.*

17. All the days of his influence, *during* which he rules, are ninety-one days.

18. And these are the signs of the days which are seen upon earth. In the days of his influence *there is* perspiration, heat, and trouble. All the trees become fruitful; the leaf of every tree comes forth; the corn is reaped; the rose and every species of flowers blossoms in the field; and the trees of winter are dried up.

19. These are the names of the conductors who are under them: Barkel, Zelsabel; and another additional conductor of a thousand is named Heloyalef, the days of whose influence have been completed. The other conductor next after them is Helemmelek, whose name they call the splendid Zahay.

20. All the days of his light are ninety-one days.

21. These are the signs of the days upon earth, heat and drought; while the trees bring forth their fruits, warmed and concocted, and give their fruits to dry.

22. The flocks follow and yean. All the fruits of the earth are collected, with everything in the fields, and the vines are trodden. This takes place during the time of his influence.

23. These are their names and orders, and *the names* of the conductors who are under them, of those who are chiefs of a thousand: Gedaeyal, Keel, Heel.

24. And the name of the additional leader of a thousand is Asphael.

25. The days of his influence have been completed.

CHAP. LXXXII. [SECT. XVI.[190]]

1. And now I have shown thee, my son Mathusala, every sight which I saw prior to thy birth.[191] I will relate another vision, which I saw before I was married; they resemble each other.

[190] Paris MS.
[191] *before thee.*

2. The first was when I was learning a book; and the other before I was married to thy mother. I saw a potent vision;

3. And on account of these things besought the Lord.

4. I was lying down in the house of my grandfather Malalel, *when* I saw in a vision heaven purifying, and snatched away.

5. And falling to the earth, I saw likewise the earth absorbed by a great abyss; and mountains suspended over mountains.

6. Hills were sinking upon hills, lofty trees were gliding[192] off from their trunks, and were in the act of being projected, and of sinking into the abyss.

7. Being alarmed at these things, my voice faltered.[193] I cried out and said, The earth is destroyed. Then my grandfather Malalel raised me up, and said to me: Why dost thou thus cry out, my son? and wherefore dost thou thus lament?

8. I related to him the whole vision which I had seen. He said to me, Confirmed is that which thou hast seen, my son;

9. And potent the vision of thy dream respecting every secret sin of the earth. Its substance shall sink into the abyss, and a great destruction take place.

10. Now, my son, rise up; and beseech the Lord of glory (for thou art faithful), that a remnant may be left upon earth, and that he would not wholly destroy it. My son, all this *calamity* upon earth comes down from heaven;[194] upon earth shall there be a great destruction.

11. Then I arose, prayed, and entreated; and wrote down my prayer for the generations of the world, explaining everything to my son Mathusala.

12. When I went out below, and looking up to heaven, beheld the sun proceeding from the east, the moon descending to the west, a few *scattered* stars, and everything which God[195] has known from the beginning, I blessed the Lord of judgment, and magnified him: because

[192] *cutting.*
[193] *the word fell down in my mouth.*
[194] *all this upon earth is from heaven.*
[195] *he.*

he hath sent forth the sun from the chambers[196] of the east; that, ascending and rising in the face of heaven, it might spring up, and pursue the path which has been pointed out to it.

CHAP. LXXXIII.

1. I lifted up my hands in righteousness, and blessed the holy, and the Great One. I spoke with the breath of my mouth, and with a tongue of flesh, which God has formed for all the sons of mortal men, that with it they may speak; giving them breath, a mouth, and a tongue to converse with.

2. Blessed art thou, O Lord, the King, great and powerful in thy greatness, Lord of all the creatures of heaven, King of kings, God of the whole world, whose reign, whose kingdom, and whose majesty endure for ever and ever.

3. From generation to generation shall thy dominion *exist*. All the heavens are thy throne for ever, and all the earth thy footstool for ever and for ever.

4. For thou hast made *them*, and over all thou reignest. No act whatsoever exceeds thy power. With thee wisdom is unchangeable; nor from thy throne and from thy presence is it ever averted. Thou knowest all things, seest and hearest them; nor is anything concealed from thee; for thou perceivest all things.

5. The angels of thy heavens have transgressed; and on mortal flesh shall thy wrath remain,[197] until the day of the great judgment.

6. Now then, O God, Lord and mighty King, I entreat thee, and beseech thee to grant my prayer, that a posterity may be left to me on earth, and that the whole human race may not perish;

7. That the earth may not be left destitute, and destruction take place for ever.

[196] *windows.*
[197] *be.*

8. O my Lord, let the race perish from off the earth which has offended thee, but a righteous and upright race establish for a posterity[198] for ever. Hide not thy face, O Lord, from the prayer of thy servant.

CHAP. LXXXIV. [SECT. XVII.[199]]

1. After this I saw another dream, and explained it all to thee, my son. Enoch arose and said to his son Mathusala, To thee, my son, will I speak. Hear my word; and incline thine ear to the visionary dream of thy father. Before I married thy mother Edna, I saw a vision on my bed;

2. And behold, a cow sprung forth from the earth;

3. And this cow was white.

4. Afterwards a female heifer sprung forth; and with it another heifer:[200] one of them was black, and one was red.[201]

5. The black heifer then struck the red one, and pursued it over the earth.

6. From that period I could see nothing more of the red heifer; but the black one increased in bulk, and a female heifer came with him.

7. After this I saw that many cows proceeded forth, resembling him, and following after him.

8. The first female young one also went out in the presence of the first cow; and sought the red heifer; but found him not.

9. And she lamented with a great lamentation, while she was seeking him.

10. Then I looked until that first *cow* came to her, from which time she became silent, and ceased to lament.

11. Afterwards she calved another white cow.

12. And again calved many cows and black heifers.

---

[198] *the plant of a seed.*
[199] Paris MS.
[200] The sense seems to require that the passage should be, "*two other heifers.*"
[201] Cain and Abel.

13. In my sleep also I perceived a white bull, which in like manner grew, and became a large white bull.

14. After him many white cows came forth, resembling him.

15. And they began to calve many *other* white cows, which resembled them and followed each other.

CHAP. LXXXV.

1. Again I looked attentively,[202] while sleeping, and surveyed heaven above.

2. And behold a single star fell from heaven.

3. Which being raised up, ate and fed among those cows.

4. After that I perceived *other* large and black cows; and behold all of them changed their stalls and pastures, while their young began to lament one with another. Again I looked in my vision, and surveyed heaven; when behold I saw many stars which descended, and projected themselves from heaven to where the first star was,

5. Into the midst of those young ones; while the cows were with them, feeding in the midst of them.

6. I looked at and observed them; when behold, they all acted after the manner of horses, and began to approach the young cows, all of whom became pregnant, and brought forth elephants, camels, and asses.

7. At these all the cows were alarmed and terrified; when they began biting with their teeth, swallowing, and striking with their horns.

8. They began also to devour the cows; and behold all the children of the earth trembled, shook with terror at them, and suddenly fled away.

[202] *with my eyes.*

CHAP. LXXXVI.

1. Again I perceived them, when they began to strike and to swallow each other; and the earth cried out. Then I raised my eyes a second time towards heaven, and saw in a vision, that, behold, there came forth from heaven as it were the likeness of white men. One came forth from thence, and three with him.

2. Those three, who came forth last, seized me by my hand; and raising me up from the generations of the earth, elevated me to a high station.

3. Then they showed me a lofty tower on the earth, while every hill became diminished. And they said, Remain here, until thou perceivest what shall come upon those elephants, camels, and asses, upon the stars, and upon all the cows.

CHAP. LXXXVII.

1. Then I looked at that one of the four *white men*, who came forth first.

2. He seized the first star which fell down from heaven.

3. And, binding it hand and foot, he cast it into a valley; a valley narrow, deep, stupendous, and gloomy.

4. Then one of them drew his sword, and gave it to the elephants, camels, and asses, who began to strike each other. And the whole earth shook on account of them.

5. And when I looked in the vision, behold, one of those four angels, who came forth, hurled from heaven, collected together, and took all the great stars, whose form partly resembled that of horses; and binding them all hand and foot, cast them into the cavities of the earth.

CHAP. LXXXVIII.

1. Then one of those four went to the white cows, and taught them a mystery. While the cow was trembling, it was born, and became a

man,[203] and fabricated for himself a large ship. In this he dwelt, and three cows[204] dwelt with him in that ship, which covered them.

2. Again I lifted up my eyes towards heaven, and saw a lofty roof. Above it were seven cataracts, which poured forth on a certain village much water.

3. Again I looked, and behold there were fountains open on the earth in that large village.

4. The water began to boil up, and rose over the earth; so that the village was not seen, while its whole soil was covered with water.

5. Much water was over it, darkness, and clouds. Then I surveyed the height of this water; and it was elevated above the village.

6. It flowed over the village, and stood higher than the earth.

7. Then all the cows which were collected there, while I looked on them, were drowned, swallowed up, and destroyed in the water.

8. But the ship floated above it. All the cows, the elephants, the camels, and the asses, were drowned on the earth, and all cattle. Nor could I perceive them. Neither were they able to get out, but perished, and sunk into the deep.

9. Again I looked in the vision until those cataracts from that lofty roof were removed, and the fountains of the earth became equalized, while other depths were opened;

10. Into which the water began to descend, until the dry ground appeared.

11. The ship remained on the earth; the darkness receded; and it became light.

12. Then the white cow, which became a man, went out of the ship, and the three cows with him.

---

[203] Noah.
[204] Shem, Ham, and Japheth.

13. One of the three cows was white, resembling that cow; one of them was red as blood; and one of them was black. And the white cow left them.

14. Then began wild beasts and birds to bring forth.

15. Of all these the different kinds assembled together, lions, tigers, wolves, dogs, wild boars, foxes, rabbits, and the hanzar,

16. The siset, the avest, kites, the phonkas, and ravens.

17. Then a white cow[205] was born in the midst of them.

18. And they began to bite each other; when the white cow, which was born in the midst of them, brought forth a wild ass and a white cow at the same time, and *after that* many wild asses. Then the white cow,[206] which was born, brought forth a black wild sow and a white sheep.[207]

19. That wild sow also brought forth many swine;

20. And that sheep brought forth twelve sheep.[208]

21. When those twelve sheep grew up, they delivered one of them[209] to the asses.[210]

22. Again those asses delivered that sheep to the wolves;[211]

23. And he grew up in the midst of them.

24. Then the Lord brought the eleven *other* sheep, that they might dwell and feed with him in the midst of the wolves.

25. They multiplied, and there was abundance of pasture for them.

26. But the wolves began to frighten and oppress them, while they destroyed their young ones.

27. And they left their young in torrents of deep water.

---

[205] Abraham.
[206] Isaac.
[207] Esau and Jacob.
[208] The twelve Patriarchs.
[209] Joseph.
[210] The Midianites.
[211] The Egyptians.

28. Now the sheep began to cry out on account of their young, and fled for refuge to their Lord. One[212] however, which was saved, escaped, and went away to the wild asses.

29. I beheld the sheep moaning, crying, and petitioning their Lord,

30. With all their might, until the Lord of the sheep descended at their voice from his lofty habitation; went to them; and inspected them.

31. He called to that sheep which had secretly stolen away from the wolves, and told him to make the wolves understand that they were not to touch the sheep.

32. Then that sheep went to the wolves with the word of the Lord, when another met him,[213] and proceeded with him.

33. Both of them together entered the dwelling of the wolves; and conversing with them made them understand, that from thenceforwards they were not to touch the sheep.

34. Afterwards I perceived the wolves greatly prevailing over the sheep with their whole force. The sheep cried out; and their Lord came to them.

35. He began to strike the wolves, who commenced a grievous lamentation; but the sheep were silent, nor from that time did they cry out.

36. I then looked at them, until they departed from the wolves. The eyes of the wolves were blind, who went out and followed them with all their might. But the Lord of the sheep proceeded with them, and conducted them.

37. All his sheep followed him.

38. His countenance *was* terrific and splendid, and glorious was his aspect. Yet the wolves began to follow the sheep, until they overtook them in a certain lake of water.[214]

39. Then that lake became divided; the water standing up on both sides before their face.

[212] Moses.
[213] Aaron.
[214] The Red Sea.

40. And while their Lord was conducting them, he placed himself between them and the wolves.

41. The wolves however perceived not the sheep, but went into the midst of the lake, following them, and running after them into the lake of water.

42. But when they saw the Lord of the sheep, they turned to fly from before his face.

43. Then the water of the lake returned, and that suddenly, according to its nature. It became full, and was raised up, until it covered the wolves. And I saw that all of them which had followed the sheep perished, and were drowned.

44. But the sheep passed over this water, proceeding to a wilderness, which was without both water and grass. And they began to open their eyes and to see.

45. Then I beheld the Lord of the sheep inspecting them, and giving them water and grass.

46. The sheep *already mentioned* was proceeding *with them*, and conducting them.

47. And when he had ascended the top of a lofty rock, the Lord of the sheep sent him to them.

48. Afterwards I perceived their Lord standing before them, with an aspect terrific and severe.

49. And when they all beheld him, they were frightened at his countenance.

50. All of them were alarmed, and trembled. They cried out after that sheep; and to the other sheep who had been with him, and who was in the midst of them, *saying*, We are not able to stand before our Lord, or to look upon him.

51. Then that sheep who conducted them went away, and ascended the top of the rock;

52.   When the *rest of the* sheep began to grow blind, and to wander from the path which he had shown them; but he knew it not.

53.   Their Lord however was moved with great indignation against them; and when that sheep had learned *what had happened,*

54.   He descended from the top of the rock, and coming to them, found that there were many,

55. Which had become blind;

56.   And had wandered from his path. As soon as they beheld him, they feared, and trembled at his presence;

57. And became desirous of returning to their fold.

58.   Then that sheep, taking with him other sheep, went to those which had wandered.

59.   And afterwards began to kill them. They were terrified at his countenance. Then he caused those which had wandered to return; who went back to their fold.

60.   I likewise saw there in the vision, that this sheep became a man, built an house for the Lord of the sheep, and made them all stand in that house.

61.   I perceived also that the sheep which proceeded to meet this sheep, their conductor, died. I saw, too, that all the great sheep perished, while smaller ones rose up in their place, entered into a pasture, and approached a river of water.[215]

62.   Then that sheep, their conductor, who became a man, was separated from them, and died.

63.   All the sheep sought after him, and cried for him with bitter lamentation.

64.   I saw likewise that they ceased to cry after that sheep, and passed over the river of water.

---

[215] The river Jordan.

65.   And that there arose other sheep, all of whom conducted them,[216] instead of those who were dead, and who had *previously* conducted them.

66.   Then I saw that the sheep entered into a goodly place, and a territory delectable and glorious.

67.   I saw also that they became satiated; that their house was in the midst of a delectable territory: and that sometimes their eyes were opened, and that sometimes they were blind; until another sheep[217] arose and conducted them. He brought them all back; and their eyes were opened.

68. Then dogs, foxes, and wild boars began to devour them, until *again* another sheep[218] arose, the master of the flock, one of themselves, a ram, to conduct them. This ram began to butt on every side those dogs, foxes, and wild boars, until they all perished.

69.   But the *former* sheep opened his eyes, and saw the ram in the midst of them, who had laid aside his glory.

70.   And he began to strike the sheep, treading upon them, and behaving himself without dignity.

71. Then their Lord sent the *former* sheep *again* to a still different[219] sheep,[220] and raised him up to be a ram, and to conduct them instead of that sheep who had laid aside his glory.

72.   Going therefore to him, and conversing with him alone, he raised up that ram, and made him a prince and leader of the flock. All the time that the dogs[221] troubled the sheep,

73. The first ram paid respect to this latter ram.

74.   Then the latter ram arose, and fled away from before his face. And I saw that those dogs caused the first ram to fall.

75. But the latter ram arose, and conducted the smaller sheep.

[216] The Judges of Israel.
[217] Samuel.
[218] Saul.
[219] *another.*
[220] David.
[221] The Philistines.

76. That ram likewise begat many sheep, and died.

77. Then there was a smaller sheep,[222] a ram, instead of him, which became a prince and leader, conducting the flock.

78. And the sheep increased in size, and multiplied.

79. And all the dogs, foxes, and wild boars feared, and fled away from him.

80. That ram also struck and killed all the wild beasts, so that they could not again prevail in the midst of the sheep, nor at any time ever snatch them away.

81. And that house was made large and wide; a lofty tower being built upon it by the sheep, for the Lord of the sheep.

82. The house was low, but the tower was elevated and very high.

83. Then the Lord of the sheep stood upon that tower, and caused a full table to approach before him.

84. Again I saw that those sheep wandered, and went various ways, forsaking that their house;

85. And that their Lord called to some among them, whom he sent[223] to them.

86. But these the sheep began to kill. And when one of them was saved from slaughter,[224] he leaped, and cried out against those who were desirous of killing him.

87. But the Lord of the sheep delivered him from their hands, and made him ascend to him, and remain with him.

88. He sent also many others to them, to testify, and with lamentations to exclaim against them.

89. Again I saw, when some of them forsook the house of their Lord, and his tower; wandering on all sides, and growing blind,

[222] Solomon.
[223] The prophets.
[224] Elijah.

90.   I saw that the Lord of the sheep made a great slaughter among them in their pasture, until they cried out to him in consequence of that slaughter. Then he departed from the place *of his habitation*, and left them in the power of lions, tigers, wolves, and the zeebt, and in the power of foxes, and of every beast.

91. And the wild beasts began to tear them.

92.   I saw, too, that he forsook the house of their fathers, and their tower; giving them all into the power of lions to tear and devour them; into the power of every beast.

93.   Then I began to cry out with all my might, imploring the Lord of the sheep, and showing him how the sheep were devoured by all the beasts of prey.

94.   But he looked on in silence, rejoicing that they were devoured, swallowed up, and carried off; and leaving them in the power of every beast for food. He called also seventy shepherds, and resigned to them *the care of* the sheep, that they might overlook them;

95.   Saying to them and to their associates, Every one of you henceforwards overlook the sheep, and whatsoever I command you, do; and I will deliver them to you numbered.[225]

96.   I will tell you which of them shall be slain; these destroy. And he delivered the sheep to them.

97.   Then he called to another, and said, Understand, and watch everything which the shepherds shall do to these sheep; for many more of them shall perish than I have commanded.

98. Of every excess and slaughter, which the shepherds shall commit, *there shall be* an account; as, how many may have perished by my command, and how many they may have destroyed of their own heads.

99.   Of all the destruction *brought about by* each of the shepherds there shall be an account; and according to the number I will cause a recital to be made before me, how many they have destroyed of their own heads,

---

[225] *with number.*

and how many they have delivered up to destruction, that I may have this testimony against them; that I may know all their proceedings; and that, delivering *the sheep* to them, I may see what they will do; whether they will act as I have commanded them, or not.

100.   *Of this*, however, they shall be ignorant; neither shalt thou make any explanation to them, neither shalt thou reprove them; but there shall be an account of all the destruction *done* by them in their respective seasons. Then they began to kill, and destroy more than it was commanded them.

101.   And they left the sheep in the power of lions, so that very many of them were devoured and swallowed up by lions and tigers; and wild boars preyed upon them. That tower they burnt, and overthrew that house.

102.   Then I grieved extremely on account of the tower, and because the house of the sheep was overthrown.

103.   Neither was I afterwards able to perceive whether they *again* entered that house.

104.   The shepherds likewise, and their associates, delivered them to all the wild beasts, that they might devour them. Each of them in his season, according to his number, was delivered up; each of them, one with another, was described in a book, how many of them, one with another, were destroyed, in a book.

105.   More, however, than was ordered, every *shepherd* killed and destroyed.

106.   Then I began to weep, and was greatly indignant, on account of the sheep.

107.   In like manner also I saw in the vision him who wrote, how he wrote down one, destroyed by the shepherds, every day. He ascended, remained, and exhibited each of his books to the Lord of the sheep, *containing* all which they had done, and all which each of them had made away with;

108. And all which they had delivered up to destruction.

109. He took the book up in his hands, read it, sealed it, and deposited it.

110. After this, I saw shepherds overlooking for twelve hours.

111.   And behold three of the sheep[226] departed, arrived, went in; and began building all which was fallen down of that house.

112. But the wild boars[227] hindered them, although they prevailed not.

113.   Again they began to build as before, and raised up that tower, which was called a lofty tower.

114.   And again they began to place before the tower a table, with every impure and unclean kind of bread upon it.

115.   Moreover also all the sheep were blind, and could not see; as were the shepherds likewise.

116.   Thus were they delivered up to the shepherds for a great destruction, who trod them under foot, and devoured them.

117.   Yet was their Lord silent, until all the sheep in the field were destroyed. The shepherds and the sheep were all mixed together; but they did not save them from the power of the beasts.

118.   Then he who wrote the book ascended, exhibited it, and read it at the residence of the Lord of the sheep. He petitioned him for them, and prayed, pointing out every act of the shepherds, and testifying before him against them all. Then taking the book, he deposited it with him, and departed.

CHAP. LXXXIX.

1. And I observed during the time, that thus thirty-seven[228] shepherds were overlooking, all of whom finished in their respective periods as the first. Others then received them into their hands, that they might overlook them in their respective periods, every shepherd in his own period.

[226] Zerubbabel, Joshua, and Nehemiah.
[227] The Samaritans.
[228] An apparent error for *thirty-five*. See verse 7. The kings of Judah and Israel.

2. Afterwards I saw in the vision, that all the birds of heaven arrived; eagles, the avest, kites and ravens. The eagle instructed them all.

3. They began to devour the sheep, to peck out their eyes, and to eat up their bodies.

4. The sheep then cried out; for their bodies were devoured by the birds.

5. I also cried out, and groaned in my sleep against that shepherd which overlooked the flock.

6. And I looked, while the sheep were eaten up by the dogs, by the eagles, and by the kites. They neither left them their body, nor their skin, nor their muscles, until their bones alone remained; until their bones fell upon the ground. And the sheep became diminished.

7. I observed likewise during the time, that twenty-three shepherds[229] were overlooking; who completed in their respective periods fifty-eight periods.

8. Then were small lambs born of those white sheep; who began to open their eyes and to see, crying out to the sheep.

9. The sheep, however, cried not out to them, neither did they hear what they uttered to them; but were deaf, blind, and obdurate in the greatest degrees.

10. I saw in the vision that ravens flew down upon those lambs;

11. That they seized one of them; and that tearing the sheep in pieces, they devoured them.

12. I saw also, that horns grew upon those lambs; and that the ravens lighted down upon their horns.

13. I saw, too, that a large horn sprouted out on an animal[230] among the sheep, and that their eyes were opened.

14. He looked at them. Their eyes were wide open; and he cried out to them.

---

[229] The kings of Babylon, etc., during and after the captivity. The numbers thirty-*five* and twenty-three make fifty-eight; and not thirty-*seven*, as erroneously put in the first verse.
[230] on *one*.

15. Then the dabela[231] saw him; all of whom ran to him.

16. And besides this, all the eagles, the avest, the ravens and the kites, were still carrying off the sheep, flying down upon them, and devouring them. The sheep were silent, but the dabela lamented and cried out.

17. Then the ravens contended, and struggled with them.

18. They wished among them to break his horn; but they prevailed not over him.

19. I looked on them, until the shepherds, the eagles, the avest, and the kites came.

20. Who cried out to the ravens to break the horn of the dabela; to contend with him; and to kill him. But he struggled with them, and cried out, that help might come to him.

21. Then I perceived that the man came who had written down the names of the shepherds, and who ascended up before the Lord of the sheep.

22. He brought assistance, and caused every one to see him descending to the help of the dabela.

23. I perceived likewise that the Lord of the sheep came to them in wrath, while all those who saw him fled away; all fell down in his tabernacle before his face; while all the eagles, the avest, ravens, and kites assembled, and brought with them all the sheep of the field.

24. All came together, and strove to break the horn of the dabela.

25. Then I saw, that the man, who wrote the book at the word of the Lord, opened the book of destruction, of that destruction which the last twelve shepherds[232] wrought; and pointed out before the Lord of the sheep, that they destroyed more than those who preceded them.

26. I saw also that the Lord of the sheep came to them, and taking in his hand the sceptre of his wrath seized the earth, which became rent asunder; while all the beasts and birds of heaven fell from the sheep, and sunk into the earth, which closed over them.

[231] The ibex, probably symbolizing Alexander the Great.
[232] The native princes of Judah after its delivery from the Syrian yoke.

27.   I saw, too, that a large sword was given to the sheep, who went forth against all the beasts of the field to slay them.

28.   But all the beasts and birds of heaven fled away from before their face.

29. And I saw a throne erected in a delectable land;

30.   Upon this sat the Lord of the sheep, who received all the sealed books;

31. Which were open before him.

32.   Then the Lord called the first seven white ones, and commanded them to bring before him the first of the first stars, which preceded the stars whose form partly resembled that of horses; the first star, which fell down first; and they brought them all before him.

33. And he spoke to the man who wrote in his presence, who was one of the seven white ones, saying, Take those seventy shepherds, to whom I delivered up the sheep, and who receiving them killed more of them than I commanded. Behold, I saw them all bound, and all standing before him. First came on the trial of the stars, which, being judged, and found guilty, went to the place of punishment. They thrust them into *a place*, deep, and full of flaming fire, and full of pillars of fire. Then the seventy shepherds were judged, and being found guilty, were thrust into the flaming abyss.

34.   At that time likewise I perceived, that one abyss was thus opened in the midst of the earth, which was full of fire.

35.   And to this were brought the blind sheep; which being judged, and found guilty, were all thrust into that abyss of fire on the earth, and burnt.

36. The abyss was on the right of that house.

37. And I saw the sheep burning, and their bones consuming.

38.   I stood beholding him immerge that ancient house, while they brought out its pillars, every plant in it, and the ivory infolding it. They brought it out, and deposited it in a place on the right side of the earth.

39.   I also saw, that the Lord of the sheep produced a new house, great, and loftier than the former, which he bounded by the former circular spot. All its pillars were new, and its ivory new, as well as more abundant than the former ancient *ivory*, which he had brought out.

40.   And while all the sheep which were left were in the midst of it, all the beasts of the earth, and all the birds of heaven, fell down and worshipped them, petitioning them, and obeying them in everything.

41.   Then those three, who were clothed in white, and who, holding me by my hand, had before caused me to ascend, while the hand of him *who* spoke held me; raised me up, and placed me in the midst of the sheep, before the judgment took place.

42.   The sheep were all white, with wool long and pure. Then all who had perished, and had been destroyed, every beast of the field, and every bird of heaven, assembled in that house: while the Lord of the sheep rejoiced with great joy, because all were good, and had come back again to his dwelling.

43.   And I saw that they laid down the sword which had been given to the sheep, and returned it to his house, sealing it up in the presence of the Lord.

44.   All the sheep would have been inclosed in that house, had it been capable of containing them;[233] and the eyes of all were open, gazing on the good One; nor was there one among them who did not behold him.

45.   I likewise perceived that the house was large, wide, and extremely full. I saw, too, that a white cow was born, whose horns were great; and that all the beasts of the field, and all the birds of heaven, were alarmed at him, and entreated him at all times.

46.   Then I saw that the nature of all of them was changed, and that they became white cows;

47. And that the first, *who* was in the midst of them, spoke,[234] when that word became a large beast, upon the head of which were great and black horns;

[233] *were inclosed in that house, and it did not contain them.*
[234] *became a word.*

48.   While the Lord of the sheep rejoiced over them, and over all the cows.

49.   I lay down in the midst of them: I awoke; and saw the whole. This is the vision which I saw, lying down and waking. Then I blessed the Lord of righteousness, and gave glory to Him.

50.   Afterwards I wept abundantly, nor did my tears cease, so that I became incapable of enduring it. While I was looking on, they flowed[235] on account of what I saw; for all was come and gone by; every individual circumstance respecting the conduct of mankind was seen by me.

51.   In that night I remembered my former dream; and therefore wept and was troubled, because I had seen that vision.

CHAP. XC. [SECT. XVIII.[236]]

1. And now, my son Mathusala, call to me all thy brethren, and assemble for me all the children of thy mother; for a voice calls me, and the spirit is poured out upon me, that I may show you everything which shall happen to you for ever.

2. Then Mathusala went, called to him all his brethren, and assembled his kindred.

3. And conversing with all his children in truth,

4. *Enoch* said, Hear, my children, every word of your father, and listen in uprightness to the voice of my mouth; for I would gain your attention, while I address you. My beloved, be attached to integrity, and walk in it.

5. Approach not integrity with a double heart; nor be associated with double-minded men: but walk, my children, in righteousness, which will conduct you in good paths; and be truth your companion.

6. For I know, that oppression will exist and prevail on earth; that on earth great punishment shall in the end take place; and that there shall be a consummation of all iniquity, which shall be cut off from its root,

[235] *descended.*
[236] Paris MS.

and every fabric *raised by* it shall pass away. Iniquity, however, shall again be renewed, and consummated on earth. Every act of crime, and every act of oppression and impiety, shall be a second time embraced.

7. When therefore iniquity, sin, blasphemy, tyranny, and every *evil* work, shall increase, and *when* transgression, impiety, and uncleanness also shall increase, *then* upon them all shall great punishment be inflicted from heaven.

8. The holy Lord shall go forth in wrath, and upon them all shall great punishment from heaven be inflicted.[237]

9. The holy Lord shall go forth in wrath, and with punishment, that he may execute judgment upon earth.

10. In those days oppression shall be cut off from its roots, and iniquity with fraud shall be eradicated, perishing from under heaven.

11. Every place of strength[238] shall be surrendered with its inhabitants; with fire shall it be burnt. They shall be brought from every part of the earth, and be cast into a judgment of fire. They shall perish in wrath, and by a judgment overpowering them[239] for ever.

12. Righteousness shall be raised up from slumber; and wisdom shall be raised up, and conferred upon them.

13. Then shall the roots of iniquity be cut off; sinners perish by the sword; and blasphemers be annihilated everywhere.[240]

14. Those who meditate oppression, and those who blaspheme, by the sword shall perish.[241]

15. And now, my children, I will describe and point out to you the path of righteousness and the path of oppression.

[237] This verse is wanting in the Paris MS. as transcribed by Woide. It seems in the Bodleian MS. to be a mere lapse of the transcriber, who wrote the same words twice over.
[238] *tower, palace,* or *temple.*
[239] *powerful judgment.*
[240] *cut off.*
[241] Between the 14th and 15th verses of this chapter six others are inserted both in the Bodleian and Paris MSS., which I have transposed so as to constitute the 13th, 14th, 15th, 16th, 17th, and 18th verses of the ninety-second chapter. This transposition seemed absolutely necessary to make sense of that chapter; in which, after the enumeration of seven weeks, or periods, the account of the eighth, ninth, and tenth weeks, contained in the verses transposed, seemed necessary to complete the narrative. Here they are clearly unconnected and misplaced.

16.   I will again point them out to you, that you may know what is to come.

17.   Here now, my children, and walk in the path of righteousness, but shun that of oppression; for all who walk in the path of iniquity shall perish for ever.

CHAP. XCI. [SECT. XIX.[242]]

1. That which was written by Enoch. He wrote all this instruction of wisdom for every man of dignity, and every judge of the earth; for all my children who shall dwell upon earth, and for subsequent generations, conducting themselves uprightly and peaceably.

2. Let not your spirit be grieved on account of the times; for the holy, the Great One, has prescribed a period[243] to all.

3. Let the righteous man arise from slumber; let him arise, and proceed in the path of righteousness, in all its paths; and let him advance[244] in goodness and in eternal clemency. Mercy shall be showed to the righteous man; upon him shall be conferred integrity and power for ever. In goodness and in righteousness shall he exist, and shall walk in everlasting light; but sin shall perish in eternal darkness, nor be seen from this time forward for evermore.

CHAP. XCII.

1. After this, Enoch began to speak from a book.

2. And Enoch said, Concerning the children of righteousness, concerning the elect of the world, and concerning the plant of righteousness and integrity.

3. *Concerning* these things will I speak, and *these things* will I explain to you, my children: I *who* am Enoch. In consequence of that which has been shown to me, from my heavenly vision and from the voice of the

[242] Paris MS.
[243] *has given days.*
[244] *his goings* be.

holy angels have I acquired knowledge; and from the tablet of heaven have I acquired understanding.

4. Enoch then began to speak from a book, and said, I have been born the seventh in the first week, while judgment and righteousness wait with patience.

5. But after me, in the second week, great wickedness shall arise, and fraud shall spring forth.

6. In that week[245] the end of the first shall take place, in which mankind shall be safe.

7. But when *the first* is completed,[246] iniquity shall grow up; and he shall execute the decree upon sinners.[247]

8. Afterwards, in the third week, during its completion, a man[248] of the plant of righteous judgment shall be selected; and after him the plant of righteousness shall come for ever.

9. Subsequently, in the fourth week, during its completion, the visions of the holy and the righteous shall be seen, the order of generation after generation *shall take place*, and an habitation shall be made for them.[249] Then in the fifth week, during its completion, the house of glory and of dominion[250] shall be erected for ever.

10.   After that, in the sixth week, all those who are in it shall be darkened, the hearts of all of them shall be forgetful of wisdom, and in it shall a man[251] ascend.

11.   And during its completion he shall burn the house of dominion with fire, and all the race of the elect root shall be dispersed.[252]

12.   Afterwards, in the seventh week, a perverse generation shall arise; abundant shall be its deeds, and all its deeds perverse. During its completion, the righteous shall be selected from the everlasting plant of

[245] *in it.*
[246] *after it has been completed.*
[247] The deluge.
[248] Abraham.
[249] The Law.
[250] Temple of Solomon.
[251] Nebuchadnezzar.
[252] Babylonian captivity.

righteousness; and to them shall be given the sevenfold doctrine of his whole creation.

13. Afterwards there shall be another week, the eighth of righteousness, to which shall be given a sword to execute judgment and justice upon all oppressors.

14. Sinners shall be delivered up into the hands of the righteous, who during its completion shall acquire habitations by their righteousness; and the house of the great King shall be established for celebrations for ever. After, this, in the ninth week, shall the judgment of righteousness be revealed to the whole world.

15. Every work of the ungodly shall disappear from the whole earth; the world shall be marked for destruction; and all men shall be on the look out for the path of integrity.

16. And after this, on the seventh day of the tenth week, there shall be an everlasting judgment, which shall be executed upon the Watchers; and a spacious eternal heaven shall spring forth in the midst of the angels.

17. The former heaven shall depart and pass away; a new heaven shall appear; and all the celestial powers shine with sevenfold splendour for ever. Afterwards likewise shall there be many weeks, which shall externally exist in goodness and in righteousness.

18. Neither shall sin be named there for ever and for ever.[253]

19. Who is there of all the children of men, capable of hearing the voice of the Holy One without emotion?

20. Who is there capable of thinking his thoughts? Who capable of contemplating all the workmanship of heaven? Who of comprehending the deeds of heaven?

21. He may behold its animation, but not its spirit. He may be capable of conversing *respecting it*, but not of ascending *to it*. He may see all the boundaries of these things, and meditate upon them; but he can make nothing like them.

---

[253] The preceding six verses, viz. 13th, 14th, 15th, 16th, 17th, and 18th, are taken from between the 14th and 15th verses of the nineteenth chapter, where they are to be found in the MSS. But the sense in this place seemed so manifestly to require them here, that I have ventured to transpose them.

22.　Who of all men is able to understand the breadth and length of the earth?

23.　By whom have been seen the dimensions of all these things? Is it every man who is capable of comprehending the extent of heaven; what its elevation is, and by what it is supported?

24.　How many are the numbers of the stars; and where all the luminaries remain at rest?

CHAP. XCIII.

1. And now let me exhort you, my children, to love righteousness, and to walk in it; for the paths of righteousness are worthy of acceptation; but the paths of iniquity shall suddenly fail, and be diminished.

2. To men of note in their generation the paths of oppression and death are revealed; but they keep far from them, and do not follow them.

3. Now, too, let me exhort you *who are* righteous, not to walk in the paths of evil and oppression, nor in the paths of death. Approach them not, that you may not perish; but covet,

4. And choose for yourselves righteousness, and a good life.

5. Walk in the paths of peace, that you may live, and be found worthy. Retain my words in your inmost thoughts, and obliterate them not from your hearts; for I know that sinners counsel men to commit crime craftily. They are not found in every place, nor does every counsel possess a little of them.

6. Woe to those who build up iniquity and oppression, and who lay the foundation of fraud; for suddenly shall they be subverted, and never obtain peace.

7. Woe to those who build up their houses with crime; for from their very foundations shall their houses[254] be demolished, and by the sword shall they *themselves* fall. Those, too, who acquire gold and silver, shall justly and suddenly perish. Woe to you who are rich, for in your riches have

[254] *they.*

you trusted; but from your riches you shall be removed; because you have not remembered the Most High in the days of your prosperity: [you shall be removed, because you have not remembered the Most High in the days of your prosperity.[255]]

8. You have committed blasphemy and iniquity; and. are destined to the day of the effusion of blood, to the day of darkness, and to the day of the great judgment.

9. This I declare and point out to you, that he who created you will destroy you.

10. When you fall, he will not show you mercy; but your Creator will rejoice in your destruction.

11. Let those, then, who shall be righteous among you in those days, detest sinners, and the ungodly.

CHAP. XCIV.

1. O that my eyes were clouds of water, that I might weep over you, and pour forth my tears like rain,[256] and rest from the sorrow of my heart!

2. Who has permitted you to hate and to transgress? Judgment shall overtake you, ye sinners.

3. The righteous shall not fear the wicked; because God will again bring them into your power, that you may avenge yourselves of them according to your pleasure.

4. Woe to you who shall be so bound by execrations, that you cannot be released from them; the remedy being far removed from you on account of your sins. Woe to you who recompense your neighbour with evil; for you shall be recompensed according to your works.

5. Woe to you, ye false witnesses, you who aggravate iniquity; for you shall suddenly perish.

---

[255] These lines are evidently a repetition of the preceding, from an error in the transcription. They do not occur in the Paris 14 MS.
[256] *a cloud of water.*

6. Woe to you, ye sinners; for you reject the righteous; for you receive or reject *at pleasure* those who *commit* iniquity; and their yoke shall prevail over you.

CHAP. XCV.

1. Wait in hope, ye righteous; for suddenly shall sinners perish from before you, and you shall exercise dominion over them, according to your will.

2. In the day of the sufferings of sinners your offspring shall be elevated, and lifted up like eagles. Your nest shall be more exalted than that of the avest; you shall ascend, and enter into the cavities of the earth, and into the clefts of the rocks for ever, like conies, from the sight of the ungodly;

3. Who shall groan over you, and weep like sirens.

4. You shall not fear those who trouble you; for restoration shall be yours; a splendid light shall shine around you, and the voice of tranquillity shall be heard from heaven. Woe to you, sinners; for your wealth makes you resemble saints, but your hearts reproach you, *knowing* that you are sinners. This word shall testify against you, for the remembrance of crime.

5. Woe to you who feed upon the glory of the corn, and drink the strength of the deepest spring,[257] and in *the pride of* your power tread down the humble.

6. Woe to you who drink water at pleasure;[258] for suddenly shall you be recompensed, consumed, and withered, because you have forsaken the fountain of life.

7. Woe to you who act iniquitously, fraudulently, and blasphemously; there shall be a remembrance against you for evil.

8. Woe to you, ye powerful, who with power strike down righteousness; for the day of your destruction shall come; *while* at that very time many

---

[257] *of the root of the spring.*
[258] *at all times.*

and good days shall be the portion of the righteous,[259] *even* at the period of your judgment.

CHAP. XCVI.

1. The righteous are confident that sinners will be disgraced, and perish in the day of iniquity.

2. You shall yourselves be conscious of it; for the Most High will remember your destruction, and the angels shall rejoice over it. What will you do ye sinners, and where will you fly in the day of judgment, when you shall hear the words of the prayer of the righteous?

3. You are not like them who in this respect witness against you; you are associates of sinners.

4. In those days shall the prayers of the righteous come up before the Lord. When the day of your judgment shall arrive; and every circumstance of your iniquity be related before the great and the holy One;

5. Your faces shall be covered with shame; while every deed, strengthened by crime, shall be rejected.

6. Woe unto you, sinners, who in the midst of the sea, and on dry land, are those against whom an evil record exists. Woe to you who squander silver and gold, not obtained in righteousness, and say, We are rich, possess wealth, and have acquired everything which we can desire.

7. Now then will we do whatsoever we are disposed to do; for we have amassed silver; our barns are full, and the husbandmen of our families are like overflowing water.[260]

8. Like water shall your falsehood pass away; for your wealth will not be permanent, but shall suddenly ascend from you, because you have obtained it all iniquitously; to extreme malediction shall you be delivered up.

---

[259] *shall come to the righteous.*
[260] *like much water.*

9. And now I swear to you, ye crafty, as well as simple ones; that you, often contemplating the earth, you *who are* men, clothe yourselves more elegantly[261] than married women, and both together more so than unmarried ones, everywhere *arraying yourselves* in majesty, in magnificence, in authority, and in silver: but gold, purple, honour, and wealth, like water, flow away.

10. Erudition therefore and wisdom are not theirs. Thus[262] shall they perish, together with their riches, with all their glory, and with their honours;

11. While with disgrace, with slaughter, and in extreme penury, shall their spirits be thrust into a furnace of fire.

12. I have sworn to you, ye sinners, that neither mountain nor hill has been or shall be subservient[263] to woman.

13. Neither in this way has crime been sent down to us[264] upon earth, but men of their own heads have invented it; and greatly shall those who give it efficiency be execrated.

14. Barrenness shall not be *previously* inflicted on woman; but on account of the work of her hands shall she die childless.

15. I have sworn to you, ye sinners, by the holy and the Great One, that all your evil deeds are disclosed in the heavens; and that none of your oppressive acts are concealed and secret.

16. Think not in your minds, neither say in your hearts, that every crime is not manifested and seen. In heaven it is daily written down before the Most High. Henceforwards shall it be manifested; for every act of oppression which you commit shall be daily recorded, until the period of your condemnation.

17. Woe to you, ye simple ones, for you shall perish in your simplicity. To the wise you will not listen, and that which is good you shall not obtain.[265]

---

[261] *put elegance upon you more.*
[262] *And in it.*
[263] *a servant.* Perhaps in furnishing them with treasures for ornaments.
[264] *has our crime been sent down.*
[265] *shall not find you.*

18.   Now therefore know that you are destined to the day of destruction; nor hope that sinners shall live; but in process of time you shall die;[266] for you are not marked[267] for redemption;

19.   But are destined to the day of the great judgment, to the day of distress, and the extreme ignominy of your souls.

20.   Woe to you, ye obdurate in heart, who commit crime, and feed on blood. Whence *is it that* you feed on good things, drink, and are satiated? Is it not because our Lord, the Most High, has abundantly supplied every good thing upon earth? To you there shall not be peace.

21.   Woe to you who love the deeds of iniquity. Why do you hope for that which is good? Know that you shall be given up into the hands of the righteous; who shall cut off your necks, slay you, and show you no compassion.

22.   Woe to you who rejoice in the trouble of the righteous; for a grave shall not be dug for you.

23.   Woe to you who frustrate the word of the righteous; for to you there shall be no hope of life.

24.   Woe to you who write down the word of falsehood, and the word of the wicked; for their falsehood they record, that they may hear and not forget folly.

25. To them there shall be no peace; but they shall surely die suddenly.

CHAP. XCVII.

1. Woe to them who act impiously, who laud and honour the word of falsehood. You have been lost in perdition; and have never led a virtuous life.

2. Woe to you who change the words of integrity. They transgress against the everlasting decree;

---

[266] *you shall go on, and die.*
[267] *pointed out.*

3. And cause the heads of those who are not sinners to be trodden down upon the earth.

4. In those days you, O ye righteous, shall have been deemed worthy of having your prayers rise up in remembrance; and shall have deposited them in testimony before the angels, that they might record the sins of sinners in the presence of the Most High.

5. In those days the nations shall he overthrown; but the families of the nations shall rise again in the day of perdition.

6. In those days they who become pregnant shall go forth, carry off their children, and forsake them. Their offspring shall slip from them, and while suckling them shall they forsake them; they shall never return to them, and never instruct their beloved.

7. Again I swear to you, ye sinners, that crime has been prepared for the day of blood, which never ceases.

8. They shall worship stones, and engrave golden, silver, and wooden images. They shall worship impure spirits, demons, and every idol, in temples; but no help shall be obtained for them.[268] Their hearts shall become impious through their folly, and their eyes be blinded with mental superstition.[269] In their visionary dreams shall they be impious and superstitious,[270] lying in all their actions, and worshipping a stone. Altogether shall they perish.

9. But in those days blessed shall they be, to whom the word of wisdom is delivered; who point out and pursue the path of the Most High; who walk in the way of righteousness, and who act not impiously with the impious.

10. They shall be saved.

11. Woe to you who expand the crime of your neighbour; for in hell shall you be slain.

12. Woe to you who lay the foundation of sin and deceit, and who are bitter on earth; for on it shall you be consumed.

---

[268] *shall be found for them.*
[269] *with the fear of their heart.*
[270] *and fear.*

13.   Woe to you who build your houses by the labour of others, every part of which is constructed with brick,[271] and with the stone of crime; I tell you, that you shall not obtain peace.

14.   Woe to you who despise the extent of the everlasting inheritance of your fathers, while your souls follow after idols; for to you there shall be no tranquillity.

15.   Woe to them who commit iniquity, and give aid to blasphemy, who slay their neighbour until the day of the great judgment; for your glory shall fall; malevolence shall He put into your hearts, and the spirit of his wrath shall stir you up, that every one of you may perish by the sword.

16. Then shall all the righteous and the holy remember your crimes.

CHAP. XCVIII.

1. In those days shall fathers be struck down with their children in the presence of each other;[272] and brethren with their brethren shall fall dead: until a river shall flow from their blood.

2. For a man shall not restrain his hand from his children, nor from his children's children; his mercy will be to kill them.[273]

3. Nor shall the sinner restrain his hand from his honoured brother. From the dawn of day to the setting sun shall the slaughter continue.[274] The horse shall wade up to his breast, and the chariot shall sink to its axle,[275] in the blood of sinners.

CHAP. XCIX.

1. In those days the angels shall descend into places of concealment, and gather together in one spot all who have assisted in crime.

---

[271] *every structure of which is brick.*
[272] *in one place.*
[273] *he has been merciful, that he may kill.*
[274] *they shall be slain.*
[275] *its upper part.*

2. In that day shall the Most High rise up to execute the great judgment upon all sinners, and to commit the guardianship of all the righteous and holy to the holy angels, that they may protect them as the apple of an eye, until every evil and every crime be annihilated.

3. Whether *or no* the righteous sleep securely,[276] wise men shall then truly perceive.

4. And the sons of the earth shall understand every word of that book, knowing that their riches cannot save them in the ruin of their crimes.

5. Woe to you, ye sinners, when you shall be afflicted on account of the righteous in the day of the great trouble; shall be burnt in the fire; and be recompensed according to your deeds.

6. Woe to you, ye perverted in heart, who are watchful to obtain an accurate knowledge of evil, and to discover terrors. No one shall assist you.

7. Woe to you, ye sinners; for with the words of your mouths, and with the work of your hands, have you acted impiously; in the flame of a blazing fire shall you be burnt.

8. And now know ye, that the angels shall inquire into your conduct in heaven; of the sun, the moon, and the stars, *shall they inquire* respecting your sins; for upon earth you exercise jurisdiction over the righteous.

9. Every cloud shall bear witness against you, the snow, the dew, and the rain: for all of them shall be withholden from you, that they may not descend upon you, nor become subservient to your crimes.

10. Now then bring gifts of salutation to the rain; that, not being withholders, it may descend upon you; and to the dew, if it has received from you gold and silver. But when the frost, snow, cold, every snowy wind, and every suffering belonging to them, fall upon you, in those days you will be utterly incapable of standing before them.

---

[276] *a deep sleep.*

CHAPTERS C-CV

CHAP. C.

1. Attentively consider heaven, all ye progeny of heaven, and all ye works of the Most High; fear him, nor conduct yourselves criminally before him.

2. If He shut up the windows of heaven, restraining the rain and dew, that it may not descend upon earth on your account, what will you do?

3. And if He send his wrath upon you, and upon all your deeds, you are not they who can supplicate him; you who utter[277] against his righteousness, language proud and powerful.[278] To you there shall be no peace.

4. Do you not see the commanders[279] of ships, how their vessels are tossed about by the waves, torn to pieces by the winds, and exposed to the greatest peril?

5. That they therefore fear, because their whole property is embarked with them on the ocean; and} that they forbode evil[280] in their hearts, because it may swallow them up, and they may perish in it?

6. Is not the whole sea, all its waters, and all its commotion, the work of him, the Most High; of him who has sealed up all its exertions, and girded it on every side with sand?

7. *Is it not* at his rebuke dried up, and alarmed; while all its fish with everything contained in it die? And will not you, ye sinners, who are on earth, fear him? Is not He the maker of heaven and earth, and of all things which are in them?

8. And who has given erudition and wisdom to all that move *progressive* upon the earth, and over the sea?

---

[277] *for you utter.*
[278] *great and powerful things.*
[279] *kings.*
[280] *think not good.*

9. Are not the commanders of ships terrified at the ocean? And shall not sinners be terrified at the Most High?

CHAP. CII[281]

1. In those days, when He shall cast the calamity of fire upon you, whither will you fly, and where will you be safe?

2. And when He sends forth his word against you, are you not spared, and terrified?

3. All the luminaries are agitated with great fear; and all the earth is spared, while it trembles, and suffers anxiety.

4. All the angels fulfil the commands *received* by them, and are desirous of being concealed from the presence of the great Glory; while the children of the earth are alarmed and troubled.

5. But you, ye sinners, are for ever accursed; to you there shall be no peace.

6. Fear not, ye souls of the righteous; but wait with patient hope for the day of your death in righteousness. Grieve not, because your souls descend in great trouble, with groaning, lamentation, and sorrow, to the receptacle of the dead. In your lifetime your bodies have not received a recompense in proportion to your goodness,[282] but in the period of your existence have sinners existed; in the period of execration and of punishment.

7. And when you die, sinners say concerning you, "As we die, the righteous die. What profit have they in their works? Behold, like us, they expire in sorrow and in darkness. What advantage have they over us? Henceforward are we equal. What will be within their grasp, and what before their eyes[283] for ever? For behold they are dead; and never will they again[284] perceive the light." I say unto you, ye sinners, You have been satiated with meat and drink, with human plunder and rapine, with sin, with the acquisition of wealth and with the sight of good days. Have

---

[281] There is no chap. ci. in the MSS.
[282] *your flesh has not found according to your goodness.*
[283] *What will they obtain, and what behold.*
[284] *henceforward for ever.*

you not marked the righteous, how their end is in peace? for no oppression is found in them even to the day of their death. They perish, and are as if they were not, while their souls descend in trouble to the receptacle of the dead.

CHAP. CIII.

1. But now I swear to you, ye righteous, by the greatness of his splendour and his glory; by his illustrious kingdom and by his majesty, to you I swear, that I comprehend this mystery; that I have read the tablet of heaven, have seen the writing of the holy Ones, and have discovered what is written and impressed on it concerning you.

2. *I have seen* that all goodness, joy, and glory has been prepared for you, and been written down for the spirits of them who die eminently righteous and good.[285] To you it shall be given in return for your troubles; and your portion *of happiness* shall far exceed the portion of the living.

3. The spirits of you who die in righteousness shall exist and rejoice. Their spirits shall exult; and their remembrance shall be before the face of the mighty One from generation to generation. Nor shall they now fear disgrace.

4. Woe to you, sinners, when you die in your sins; and they, who are like you, say respecting you, Blessed are these sinners. They have lived out their whole period;[286] and now they die in happiness[287] and in wealth. Distress and slaughter they knew not[288] while alive; in honour they die; nor ever in their lifetime did judgment overtake them.

5. *But* has it not been shown to them, that, when to the receptacle of the dead t heir souls shall be made to descend, their evil deeds shall become their greatest torment? Into darkness, into the snare, and into the flame,

---

[285] *in righteousness and in much goodness.*
[286] *They have seen all their days.*
[287] *in goodness.*
[288] *they saw not.*

which shall burn to the great judgment, shall their spirits enter; and the great judgment shall take effect for ever and for ever.[289]

6. Woe to you; for to you there shall be no peace. Neither can you say to the righteous, and to the good who are alive, "In the days of our trouble have we been afflicted; every *species of* trouble have we seen, and many evil things have suffered.[290]

7. Our spirits have been consumed, lessened, and diminished.

8. We have perished; nor has there been a possibility of help for us in word or in deed: we have found none, but have been tormented and destroyed.

9. We have not expected to live[291] day after day.

10. We hoped indeed to have been the head;

11. But we have become the tail. We have been afflicted, when we have exerted ourselves; but we have been devoured by sinners[292] and the ungodly; their yoke has been heavy upon us.

12. Those have exercised dominion over us who detest and who goad us; and to those who hate us have we humbled our neck; but they have shown no compassion towards us.

13. We have been desirous of escaping from them, that we might fly away and be at rest; but we have found no place to which we could fly, and be secure from them. We have sought an asylum with princes in our distress, and have cried out to those who were devouring us; but our cry has not been regarded, nor have they been disposed to hear our voice;

14. But rather to assist those who plunder and devour us; those who diminish us, and hide their oppression; who remove not their yoke from us, but devour, enervate, and slay us; who conceal our slaughter, nor remember that they have lifted up their hands against us."

---

[289] *shall be for every generation, even for ever.*
[290] *found.*
[291] *to see life.*
[292] *food for sinners.*

CHAP. CIV.

1. I swear to you, ye righteous, that in heaven the angels record your goodness before the glory of the mighty One.

2. Wait with patient hope; for formerly you have been disgraced with evil and with affliction; but now shall you shine like the luminaries of heaven. You shall be seen, and the gates of heaven shall be opened to you. Your cries have cried for judgment; and it has appeared to you: for an account of all your sufferings shall be required from the princes, and from every one who has assisted your plunderers.

3. Wait with patient hope; nor relinquish your confidence; for great joy shall be yours, like that of the angels in heaven. Conduct yourselves as you may, still you shall not be concealed in the day of the great judgment. You shall not be found like sinners; and eternal condemnation shall be far from you, so long as the world exists.[293]

4. And now fear not, ye righteous, when you see sinners flourishing and prosperous[294] in their ways.

5. Be not associates with them; but keep yourselves at a distance from their oppression; be you associated with the host of heaven. You, ye sinners, say, All our transgressions shall not be taken account of, and be recorded. But all your transgressions shall be recorded daily.

6. And be assured by me,[295] that light and darkness, day and night, behold all your transgressions. Be not impious in your thoughts; lie not; surrender not the word of uprightness; lie not against the word of the holy and the mighty One; glorify not your idols; for all your lying and all your impiety is not for righteousness, but for great crime.

7. Now will I point out a mystery: Many sinners shall turn and transgress against the word of uprightness.

---

[293] *during every generation of the world.*
[294] *strong and worthy.*
[295] *I will show you.*

8. They shall speak evil things; they shall utter falsehood; execute great undertakings;[296] and compose books in their own words. But when they shall write all my words correctly in their own languages,

9. They shall neither change or diminish them; but shall write them all correctly; all which from the first I have uttered concerning them.

10.   Another mystery also I point out. To the righteous and the wise shall be given books of joy, of integrity, and of great wisdom. To them shall books be given, in which they shall believe;

11.   And in which they shall rejoice. And all the righteous shall be rewarded, who from these shall acquire the knowledge of every upright path.

CHAP. CIV.[297]

1. In those days, saith the Lord, they shall call to the children of the earth, and make them listen to their wisdom. Show them that you are their leaders;

2. And that renumeration *shall take place* over the whole earth; for I and my Son will for ever hold communion with them in the paths of uprightness, while they are still alive.[298] Peace shall be yours. Rejoice, children of integrity, in the truth.

CHAP. CV.

1. After a time,[299] my son Mathusala took a wife for his son Lamech.

2. She became pregnant by him, and brought forth a child, the flesh of which was as white as snow, and red as a rose; the hair of whose head was white like wool, and long; and whose eyes were beautiful. When he opened them, he illuminated all the house, like the sun; the whole house abounded with light.

---

[296] *create a great creation.*
[297] This chapter occurs twice.
[298] *we will for ever mix with them in the paths of uprightness in their lives.*
[299] *after days.*

3. And when he was taken from the hand of the midwife, opening also his mouth, he spoke to the Lord of righteousness. Then Lamech his father was afraid of him; and flying away came to his own father Mathusala, and said, I have begotten a son, unlike *to other children*.[300] He is not human; but, resembling the offspring of the angels of heaven, is of a different nature *from ours*, being altogether unlike to us.

4. His eyes are *bright* as the rays of the sun; his countenance glorious, and he looks not as if he belonged to me, but to the angels.

5. I am afraid, lest something miraculous should take place on earth in his days.

6. And now, my father, let me entreat and request you to go to our progenitor Enoch, and to learn from him the truth; for his residence is with the angels.

7. When Mathusala heard the words of his son, he came to me at the extremities of the earth; for he had been informed that I was there: and he cried out.

8. I heard his voice, and went to him saying, Behold, I am *here*, my son; since thou art come to me.

9. He answered and said, On account of a great event have I come to thee; and on account of a sight difficult *to be comprehended* have I approached thee.

10. And now, my father, hear me; for to my son Lamech a child has been born, who resembles not him; and whose nature is not like the nature of man. His colour is whiter than snow; he is redder than the rose; the hair of his head is whiter than white wool; his eyes are like the rays of the sun; and when he opened them he illuminated the whole house.

11. When also he was taken from the hand of the midwife, he opened his mouth, and blessed the Lord of heaven.

12. His father Lamech feared, and fled to me, believing not that *the child* belonged to him, but that he resembled the angels of heaven. And behold I am come to thee, that thou mightest point out to me the truth.

[300] *a changed son.*

Then I, Enoch, answered and said, The Lord will effect a new thing upon the earth. This have

I explained, and seen in a vision. I have shown thee that in the generations of Jared my father, those who were from heaven disregarded the word of the Lord. Behold they committed crimes; laid aside their class, and intermingled with women. With them also they transgressed; married with them, and begot children.

14. A great destruction therefore shall come upon all the earth; a deluge, a great destruction, shall take place in one year.

15. This child which is born to you shall survive on the earth, and his three sons shall be saved with him. When all mankind who are on earth shall die, he shall be safe.

16. And his posterity shall beget on the earth giants, not spiritual, but carnal. Upon the earth shall a great punishment be inflicted, and it shall be washed from all corruption. Now therefore inform thy son Lamech, that he who is born is his child in truth; and he shall call his name *Noah*, for he shall be to you a survivor. He and his children shall be saved from the corruption which shall take place in the world; from all the sin and from all the iniquity which shall be consummated on earth in his days. Afterwards shall greater impiety take place than that which had been before consummated on the earth; for I am acquainted with holy mysteries, which the Lord himself has discovered and explained to me; and which I have read in the tablets of heaven.

17. In them I saw it written, that generation after generation shall transgress, until a righteous race shall arise; until transgression and crime perish from off the earth; until all goodness come upon it.

18. And now, my son, go tell thy son Lamech,

19. That the child which is born is his child in truth; and that there is no deception.

20. When Mathusala heard the word of his father Enoch, who had shown hint every secret thing, he returned with understanding,[301] and called the

[301] *seeing.*

name of that child Noah; because he was to console the earth on account of all its destruction.

21. Another book, which Enoch wrote for his son Mathusala, and for those who should come after him, and preserve their purity of conduct[302] in the latter days. You, who have laboured, shall wait in those days, until the evil doers be consumed, and the power of the guilty be annihilated. Wait, until sin pass away; for their names shall be blotted out of the holy books; their seed shall be destroyed, and their spirits slain. They shall cry out and lament in the invisible waste, and in the bottomless fire shall they burn.[303] There I perceived, as it were, a cloud which could not be seen through; for from the depth of it I was unable to look upwards. I beheld also a flame of fire blazing brightly, and, as it were, glittering mountains whirled around, and agitated from side to side.

22. Then I inquired of one of the holy angels who was with me, and said, What is this splendid *object?* For it is not heaven, but a flame of fire alone which blazes; and *in it there is* the clamour of exclamation, of woe, and of great suffering.

23. He said, There, into that place which thou beholdest, shall be thrust the spirits of sinners and blasphemers; of those who shall do evil, and who shall pervert all which God has spoken by the mouth of the prophets; all which they ought to do.

For respecting these things there shall be writings and impressions above in heaven, that the angels may read them and know what shall happen both to sinners and to the spirits of the humble; to those who have suffered in their bodies, but have been rewarded by God; who have been injuriously treated by wicked men; who have loved God; who have been attached neither to gold nor silver, nor to any good thing in the world, but have given their bodies to torment;

24. To those who from the period of their birth[304] have not been covetous of earthly riches; but have regarded themselves as a breath passing away.

---

[302] *their state of life.*
[303] *in the fire shall they burn, where there is no earth.*
[304] *from the time they were.*

25. Such has been their conduct;[305] and much has the Lord tried them; and their spirits have been found pure, that they might bless his name. All their blessings have I related in a book; and He has rewarded them; for they have been found to love heaven with an everlasting aspiration. *God has said*, While they have been trodden down by wicked men, they have heard from them revilings and blasphemies; and have been ignominiously treated, while they were blessing me. And now will I call the spirits of the good from the generation of light, and will change those who have been born in darkness; who have not in their bodies been recompensed with glory, as their faith may have merited.

26. I will bring them into the splendid light of those who love my holy name: and I will place each of them on a throne of glory, of glory *peculiarly* his own, and they shall be at rest during unnumbered periods. Righteous is the judgment of God;

27. For to the faithful shall he give faith in the habitations of uprightness.[306] They shall see those, who having been born in darkness unto darkness shall be cast; while the righteous shall be at rest. Sinners shall cry out, beholding them, while they exist in splendour and proceed forwards to the days and periods prescribed to them.[307]

Here ends the vision of Enoch the prophet. May the benediction of his prayer, and the gift of his appointed period, be with his beloved! Amen.

Printed in Great Britain
by Amazon